I Love You, I Love You Too

KING SOLOMON SPIRITUAL LIBRARY
THE GOD ENCYCLOPAEDIA WORD OF INFINITY

BY
THE HOLY SPIRIT OF THE FATHER GOD
THROUGH HIS SERVANT
HRM KING SOLOMON DAVID JESSE ETE
(King Solomon Spiritual Library)
Eteroyal Universal Family -BCS

I Love You, I Love You Too

*All rights reserved
Copyright © Solomon ETE, 2008
Solomon ETE is hereby identified as author
of this work in accordance with Section 77
of the Copyright, Designs and Patents Act
1988*

*The book cover picture is copyright
to Solomon ETE*

*This book is published by
King Solomon Spiritual Library
P O BOX 27394
London E12 6WW UK
www.kingsolomonspirituallibrary.com*

This book is sold subject to the conditions that it shall not, by way of trade or otherwise, be lent, resold, hired out or otherwise circulated without the author's or publisher's prior consent in any form of binding or cover other than that in which it is published and without a similar condition including this condition being imposed on the subsequent purchaser.

A CIP record for this book is available from the British Library
ISBN 978-0-9559801-3-8

I LOVE YOU

=====

I YOU LOVE TOO

An Open Universal Love Letter

===========

THE UNIVERSAL UPDATE

======

HIDU-CUM

THE SUPREME LOVE STORY

=====

LIVE AND LET LIVE

Content

Chapter One   **7-105**

I LOVE YOU

Introduction   8-13

A: Love From The Universal Supreme Word The Father God Almighty   14-37

B: I Am Pleading With Every Human Soul   37-55

C: Through Love I Created Human Beings   55-66

D: Love Is The Only Way To Save The Whole World 67-78

E: Those Who Love Shall Be Saved   78-91

F: You Are Condemned Unless You Love   91-94

G: Love Is The Only

Remedy   94-98

Conclusion A: 99-100
Nobody Can Bypass Love

Conclusion B: 101-104
This Is Humanity's Last Chance

Conclusion C: 104-105
I Love You

Chapter Two   **106-202**

THE UNIVERSAL UPDATE

Introduction   106-117

A: Universal Update   117-123

B: What Is Going On In Your
Mind   123-133

C: Everybody Must Update His
Or Her Mind Now   134-147

D: Do Not Be Like The Little Red
Ants With Sugar   147-158

E: Every Soul Must Reconcile

With Me Or Else	159-171
F: The Time To Make Your Decision	171-176
G: Blame Yourself	176-185
Conclusion A: If You Love Your Soul Do Not Reject This Message	185-189
Conclusion B: This Is My Update To All Human Kind	190-191
Conclusion C: The Only Remedy	192-202

Chapter Three   203-213
HIDU-CUM-Love Story

Chapter Four   214-237
LIVE AND LET LIVE

With Love	**251-258**
Title List	**264-270**
Love Letter Respond	**271**

Chapter One

FATHER'S TALK
(GOD PRESENT)
Christ Our Lord, Thirteenth Bartholomew, FATHER,
Two Thousand and Eight (AC/OI/BOOH)
Saturday, Thirteenth September, Year Two Thousand and
Eight (13/09/2008)

In the name of Our Lord Jesus Christ, In the Blood of Our Lord Jesus Christ, Now and forever more

I LOVE YOU

======

I LOVE YOU TOO

An Open Universal Love Letter

THE DIVINE UNION OF

THE FATHER GOD ALMIGHTY

WITH HUMANKIND

Today, it pleases **ME, THE FATHER GOD THE CREATOR OF THE UNIVERSE, THE SUPREME WORD OF ALL THINGS** to give this wonderful Lecture Revelation titled, **I LOVE YOU – AN OPEN UNIVERSAL 'LOVE LETTER' FROM THE FATHER GOD ALMIGHTY TO ALL MANKIND.**

INTRODUCTION

This Lecture Revelation, **I AM** giving now is to bring all **MY** creation back to **MY DIVINE SELF OF LOVE.** It is called sweetness of the body because it is sweetness of the instinct. **I** use this Lecture Revelation to make those who are sick to become well. **I** use this Lecture Revelation to make

those who lack to become wealthy and have plentiful. **I** use this Lecture Revelation of today to make those who are depressed to become happy!
If you find yourself in any position that makes you unhappy because it is not good and maybe in one way or the other Satan put you in, then **I** use this Lecture Revelation to lift you up. Whatever it is, in whatever position and at wherever that you find yourself to be and you are not happy about it, **I** use this Lecture Revelation to lift you out of such an unhappy situation.

I LOVE YOU. This is a Lecture Revelation for every human soul. **I** will reveal the meaning of **I, LOVE** and **YOU,** in this Lecture Revelation.
THIS IS A SPECIAL OPEN LETTER TO ALL CHILDREN

OF GOD AND ALL HUMAN BEINGS ON EARTH.
If you are positive, you will be so happy to have this Lecture Revelation with you. If you are a human being that knows the meaning of good things and their importance in your life and the meaning of **LOVE** then you will be so glad and overwhelmed with joy and will jump with happiness and make merry about this Lecture Revelation **THE FATHER'S TALK (GOD PRESENT)**, titled **I LOVE YOU.** Why can **I** not **LOVE YOU? I AM LOVE. I AM THE WORD** in you and you in **ME** so, why should **I** not **LOVE YOU?**

I have to tell you that all the disasters, all the problems, all the predicaments, all the bad situations and woes that befall

I Love You, I Love You Too

humankind in general and you experience are not from **ME–o-oh! - THE FATHER GOD. I, THE FATHER GOD ALMIGHTY** DO NOT DESTROY ANYTHING! **I THE FATHER GOD ALMIGHTY DO NOT DESTROY ANY POSITIVE THING**. Imagine that **I** would create something and then destroy that thing. NO! **I** don't! **I** want to prove to you that **I LOVE YOU** hence **I** write this letter to you today. It is a **LOVE LETTER** to sweeten your heart. I call you **MY SWEETHEART**. I call you **SWEET BODY** and a **PERFECT PARTNER**.

And **I** change your body language that used to be evil to positive love of **GOD**.

When you have this Lecture Revelation, take it is for your

heart. **I** want you to take this Revelation Lecture and put in your chest. **I** want you to hold this Lecture Revelation to your chest and embrace it and say **I LOVE YOU,** just as **I** say to you – **I LOVE YOU.** Do you **LOVE ME?**

I THE FATHER GOD THE SUPREME WORD OF THE UNIVERSE is asking you: **MY DAUGHTER** and MY SON DO YOU **LOVE ME**? Do you **LOVE** YOUR **FATHER GOD**? Do you **LOVE THE WORD**?
Do you **LOVE LIFE**? Do you **LOVE ME?**
If you **LOVE ME** then **I LOVE YOU**.

This is **MY LETTER TO YOU** therefore, if **I** ask you, "DO YOU **LOVE ME** and you answer **ME** back with**, "I LOVE YOU"**, then

I LOVE YOU. And that is the meaning of **ONENESS**. That is the meaning of **PARTNERSHIP**. That is the meaning of **TOGETHERNESS** and **MARRIAGE**.

If **I** say to you, **I LOVE YOU**, what will you say to **ME** in response? You will say to **ME, I LOVE YOU TOO.** Will you tell **ME, I LOVE YOU TOO,** since **I LOVE YOU**? If you answer yes to all this, as **I** say to you **I LOVE YOU** and you answer **ME** that **YOU LOVE ME, THE FATHER GOD ALMIGHTY** then immediately, **MY SPIRIT OF LOVE** will be activated in you.

A: LOVE FROM THE UNIVERSAL SUPREME WORD THE FATHER GOD ALMIGHTY

I, THE FATHER GOD ALMIGHTY GIVE YOU MY LOVE. I say to all creations, especially human beings, **I LOVE YOU** and **I** require a response from you. **I AM THE ONE** sending you this **LOVE LETTER** as a Letter of Oneness, Letter of Cooperation and Letter of Peace as **A SUPREME LOVE LETTER!**
I have never sent this type of **LOVE LETTER** before since **I** created humankind on this earth, from the time of Adam. This is the letter that Lucifer rushed to come and give to Eve in the negative way, then Eve gave to Adam and

they ate the forbidden fruit. Now, what do you think this letter means? It means **EVERLASTING LIFE** to you. Nevertheless, how will you get this **EVERLASTING LIFE**? That is now the problem. If **I** say to you **I LOVE YOU,** what **I** need from you is, **I LOVE YOU TOO FATHER GOD ALMIGHTY.** And when you say you **LOVE ME,** what will happen is that, you will respect **THE SUPREME WORD OF THE UNIVERSE.** You will join in the celebration of the **SUPREME WORD** on earth, which is titled, *THE UNIVERSAL SUPREME WORD SEASON CELEBRATION.* The first thing that should come into your heart is peace because you would reason thus:

I LOVE THE FATHER GOD as **THE FATHER GOD LOVES** me.
HE has given me invitation of **LOVE**.
HE created me.
HE knows about me therefore, **LOVES** me.
HE is my brother.
HE is my sister.
HE is my husband.
HE is my wife.
HE is my friend.
HE is everything to me.
And for all this, **I** will **LOVE HIM** back. **I LOVE YOU TOO FATHER GOD ALMIGHTY.**

If you make this agreement with **ME** and say that you **LOVE ME TOO** then you are going to join in the celebration of the **SUPREME WORD** on earth. When you think about this, then you will not stand aside rather, you will come

forward and promote this program. You will come forward to help to make everywhere peaceful.
If you are a president, **I LOVE YOU.**
Do you **LOVE ME** too?
If you are a head of state, **I LOVE YOU.**
Do you **LOVE ME** too?
If you are a woman **I LOVE YOU.**
Do you **LOVE ME** too?
If you are a man, **I LOVE YOU.**
Do you **LOVE ME** too?
If you are a child **I LOVE YOU**
Do you **LOVE ME** too?
If you are a poor person, **I LOVE YOU.**
Do you **LOVE ME** too?
If you are a rich person, **I LOVE YOU.**
Do you **LOVE ME** too?

I LOVE EVERY CREATION.
Does every creation **LOVE ME** too?
If you are a king, a queen, a prime minister or anything else, **I LOVE YOU – ALL OF YOU**, since you are a human being
Do you **LOVE ME** too?
Scientist, **I LOVE YOU.**
Do you **LOVE ME** too?

I LOVE YOU! When you were born into this earth **I** did not break any of your legs. **I** did not make you to have three legs instead of two. That is how much **I LOVE YOU. I LOVE YOU** all scientist! That is the reason that when you were born into this world, **I** did not make you blind to be a blind person. **I** did not make you dumb. **I** gave you the sense of understanding. **I AM** the only science in your heart. So, why do you decide to hate **ME?** Why do you hate **ME, THE FATHER GOD** so much? You hate so-o-o, so much – so much that you change **MY** products to be artificial.

Scientists! Technologists! Do you **LOVE ME,** as **I LOVE YOU? I LOVE YOU SO MUCH** that **I** allowed you to operate.
I give you knowledge.
I give you understanding.
I let you know how to mix chemicals turn it into many things.
So, why do you hate **ME?**
I make you to be alive. **I AM THE LIFE** in **YOU.**

Look at how small you were when your mother gave birth to you but you grew and went to school and learnt many things. Why do you decide to use such a privilege to fight against **ME?** You change things that **I** made and use them to

destroy the world – **MY WORLD, MY CREATIONS**.
Why do you build nuclear weapons?
Why do you build things to use to destroy humans that **I** created just like **I** created you?
Why do you encourage bad things?
Why do you use the knowledge that **I** gave you to encourage evil?
Why do you turn good things to be evil things?

Every human being that has life, **I LOVE YOU**.
Why do you use the life that **I** give you to fight against a life like you?
Do you **LOVE ME** then? Answer this question!
I LOVE YOU, ALL HUMAN BEINGS.
Do you **LOVE ME** too?
Then answer thus:

I LOVE YOU TOO HOLY FATHER GOD ALMIGHTY, THE SUPREME WORD OF THE UNIVERSE, THE CREATOR, THE LIFE FORCE, THE ENERGY OF LIFE, I LOVE YOU TOO.
Speak like this and let your conscience be clear.

You, the judge in the law court that has judged someone knowing full well that the person you have sentenced to death is worried about dying, yet you opened your mouth and said to that person, 'I sentence you to death'. Do you **LOVE ME?** You sent a life to death. You sent the same life that you have to death.

You, who has the heart to kill someone as an armed robber carrying a gun to shoot another person because you need something, why didn't you just

take what you needed and leave the human life? Do you **LOVE ME?**
If you **LOVE ME,** you will not kill again.
If you are hungry you can just take food and eat. If everybody takes care of everybody nobody would kill anybody. What do you kill for if you **REALLY LOVE THE FATHER GOD?** Answer the question.

I LOVE YOU and **I** have forgiven you all the sins you committed. But do you **LOVE ME** to forgive one another?
I died on the cross and said, "IT IS FINISHED". **I AM THE SUPREME WORD,** the Higher Self of Adam who came and died for humankind. That is the reason **I** why **I** do not destroy the world. People capitalize on **MY** long patience and say that there is no

I Love You, I Love You Too

GOD because despite all the atrocities and evil that human beings commit, they do not see **ME, THE FATHER GOD** destroying the whole world like before. That is why they conclude that there is no **GOD** but that is **MY LOVE IN ACTION.**
I use **LOVE** to condone you.
I use **LOVE** to have patience for you to change.
I use **LOVE** to deliver this message.
I use **LOVE** to do everything on earth.
Do you **LOVE ME**? If you **LOVE ME** then you **LOVE** your life.
One of the Ten Commandments says **LOVE THY NEIGHBOUR AS THEY SELF**. Because human beings can kill themselves, it means that they do not love themselves again. That was why **I**

said, "**LOVE ONE ANOTHER AS I LOVE YOU**".

You, suicide bomber, do you **LOVE ME** too?
If you **LOVE ME,** then you should **LOVE** your life. Are you the one that gave yourself the life that you have used a bomb to terminate? Do you know how life managed to be in existence? You, that goes about charging for the air, claiming that you owe this sky to that sky. Are you sure you own that sky? Why do you go about charging for water and other amenities, when you shouldn't? All the things that **I** have done and put in place on earth are to benefit humankind. Everybody that is born into this world has the opportunity to benefit from what **THE FATHER GOD** has done. Everybody is a servant to one another. If you **LOVE** your fellow

I Love You, I Love You Too

human beings then, all is well. That means you **LOVE ME.** If **I** say to you, **"I LOVE YOU"** and you reply, **I LOVE YOU TOO**. Who do you think really love?

A woman that tells a man, **I LOVE YOU** and the man replies, **I LOVE YOU TOO,** who do you really think they **LOVE**? When someone has a sweet body for another person, what do you think happened? It is the life inside you that is responsible. Do you embrace a dead body? Can you cuddle a dead body, hold it to your chest and squeeze it like you want to enter into that person? You can't you do that to a dead body. It is the life, which is **ME, THE FATHER GOD** inside the living person that you squeeze and that is why, if **I LOVE YOU,** you must **LOVE ME.**
Do you **LOVE ME** too?

If you **LOVE ME** you will LOVE ONE ANOTHER.
If you **LOVE ME** you will LOVE to be a peacemaker.
If you **LOVE ME** you will LOVE to practice equality.
If you **LOVE ME** you will LOVE oneness and practice oneness; you will LOVE to be merciful and will practice mercy; you will LOVE to be kind and will practice kindness.
If you **LOVE ME** you will love to love your fellow human beings because **YOU LOVE ME. I LOVE YOU TOO.** You **LOVE ME** as **I LOVE YOU.**
I AM the first to **LOVE** you. Without **LOVE I** would not create humans in **MY image** and **likeness.** Does it mean that you are not happy to be a human being? You are not happy to see yourself as a human being? That is why you go about hating life.

Okay! Since you are not happy to be a human being **I** will return you to your original lower nature. If you are a human being and you practice hatred **I** will return you to a tree. If you are a human being and you hate **I** will make you to be sand. If you a human being and you hate **I** will return you to zero. You are not warranted to be a human being since you hate another human being.

Since you are not warranted to be a real human being because you hate **I** will return you to human animal or **I** will reduce you from your original template to zero. **I** will return you to something that you are capable of handling as you cannot handle being a human being. You cannot take care of another human because human beings are supposed to LOVE.

Human beings represent **THE FATHER GOD** therefore you are to take care of other junior ones but you refuse to do that. If **I** make you a President and you go to war, then over your dead body you can never be a President again in any generation. Any President with all their supporters that go to war in this Twenty-first Century, this time that the civilization of **THE FATHER GOD - THE FATHER GOD'S LOVE** has covered the earth will pay for their actions. If you are President, a Prime Minister, a King, or even an ordinary village head, in fact any position you occupy and you purposely go to war to kill someone and do all sorts of wicked things on your fellow human beings, **I** will reduce you to below zero because you are not warranted to be a human being.

You do not merit the term human being therefore **I** will send you to where you are suited.
DO YOU LOVE ME?
If you **LOVE ME** keep **MY** commandment. What is **MY** commandment? **MY** commandment is, **LOVE YE ONE ANOTHER**.
Be peaceful.
Be merciful.
Be kind.
Be nice to everybody.
Forgive one another.
Live a clean life.
Do not be a problem to anybody.
If you do not want to do that then, you give **ME** no other option than to reduce you to something that is fit for you. Since you are already an object soul **I** can give you a borrowed soul.
I could make you a fish.
I could make you a tree.

I can make you into any low – very low creation because you are not worthy to be a human being to represent **ME, THE FATHER GOD.**
All those souls who answer **I LOVE YOU TOO** and they practice **LOVE** and practice **PEACE** and are **MERCIFUL** and practice **KINDNESS** and practice **RIGHTEOUSNESS** which is **HONESTY** and they try their best to live with one another and to support one another and love one another as those who say to themselves, left to me alone there will be perfect peace in this world, these are **MY** children.

Anybody who knows himself or herself that they are not involved with the practice of witchcraft and they do not intend to be one, they do not practice wickedness of any kind, they do not join any secret society or other evil societies, rather they just live their lives as the set of people that left to them alone there would be peace in this world are the people that will rule with **ME** in **THE FATHER GOD'S SUPREME FUTURE**. These are the types of people **I** will continue to improve. And if anything happens to their lives here on earth **I** return them back on earth and make plenty copies of them that nobody can fight against.

Let **ME** tell you since **YOU LOVE ME,** as **I LOVE YOU** and you support **ME** like His Royal Majesty King Solomon David Jesse ETE who supports **ME**, you will become a promised soul as King Solomon. He **LOVES ME** and He is **MY** Servant. **I** made Him a promise and it extends to all other Servants of God. Have you not heard of the promise **I** made to Him just as **I** made to His father Adam, Abraham and to King David that his seeds would fill the earth and he would be the father of all nations? It is the same promise **I** make to HRM King Solomon David Jesse ETE who is the son of Adam, the son of Abraham and the son of King David that **I** will make seventy-two million copies of his positive selves of servant-ship to be **MY** servants to serve **THE FATHER GOD** for eternity. These copies will never fail. They will all recognize the original self and He will be the Head of all Servant-ships to serve **THE FATHER GOD.** And they will all be real Human-Gods on earth. That is the promise **I** made to Him. That is the New Covenant **I** make with

Him this day therefore, if you **LOVE ME** as **I LOVE YOU, I** will increase your copy.
I will circulate you.
I will multiply your copy for the same good job you are doing. And your real copy will continue to be the original copy and that is why **I** said, "The blessing **I** give to HRM King Solomon David Jesse ETE, **I** will not give to anybody else."

HRM King Solomon David Jesse ETE is the real copy and remains the REAL copy. And even if anything happens to His physical life **I** would use that opportunity and make millions of His copies and make Him so powerful because all those millions of copies would back Him up and fight His enemies. You will see what will happen. If you stand with The TRUTH, The TRUTH will back you up. **I AM THE**

TRUTH. If anybody points one finger at **MY** child, **I** will make ten fingers of himself or herself to point back at them and they are finished!

What is the meaning of Guardian Angel? If you come to this world once and do good things, you come back twice and do good things twice, and come back the third time and do good things three times, **I** will join all the good things to you and when you come back again, the other selves become your Guardians because all that selves are **THE FATHER GOD.** They will back you up for all the good things that you have done, are doing and will continue doing. A similar thing applies to those who do evil. When they come back their evil will follow them and if they continue to do evil then more destruction will follow them until their evil origin ends.

I AM giving this truth information to everybody. DO NOT DECEIVE ANYONE ANYMORE. This **FATHER'S TALK (GOD PRESENT)** Lecture Revelation is an eye opener. **I LOVE YOU.** If you answer **I LOVE YOU TOO**, your eyes will open right away. Read the Lecture Revelation titled: ***HIDU-CUM and seven other titles of THE FATHER'S TALK (GOD PRESENT).*** If you read *HIDU-CUM* and another seven of **THE FATHER'S TALK (GOD PRESENT)** Lecture Revelations and you have this letter, then find a way to connect to **ME, THE FATHER GOD** directly.

As **I LOVE YOU**, take **ME** as your **LOVER**.

Take **ME** as your **FATHER**.

Take **ME** as your Mother.
Take **ME** as your boyfriend and man friend.
Take **ME** as your girlfriend and woman friend.
Take **ME** as your child.
Take **ME** as your husband or wife and all other relations and friendships that are positive.
Take **ME** as everything for you because **I** have taken you as **MY** son, as **MY** daughter, as **MY** brother and as **MY** sister. Every name means a WORD and what is that? It is **THE SUPREME WORD OF THE UNIVERSE.** Nobody actually exists except **THE FATHER GOD.** And since only **THE FATHER GOD** exists, you only exist in **ME, THE FATHER GOD** in positivism. Since **I** have never had any glory in any negativism, **I AM** destroying all negativisms

therefore, if you do not exist in **ME** in **POSITIVISM,** you are finished. Therefore this is **AN OPEN LOVE LETTER FROM ME THE FATHER GOD THE UNIVERSAL SUPREME WORD.**

B: I AM PLEADING WITH EVERY HUMAN SOUL

I AM pleading with every human soul to accept **MY LOVE LETTER.** This **LOVE LETTER** surpasses all letters and love stories on earth. This is **A SUPREME LOVE LETTER** that **I** write to humankind.

This one is the update and it is above The Love Songs of Solomon. Anybody that reads this Lecture Revelation will feel the impact of the **LOVE OF THE**

FATHER GOD and will not have any problems in their married life. If you believe **THE FATHER'S TALK (GOD PRESENT)** and you read this Lecture Revelation then all spirit-souls that are disturbing your general and marriage life has ended.

If you believe the **LOVE OF GOD** in your heart and you **LOVE ME** and answered **I LOVE YOU TOO,** when **I** said to you **I LOVE YOU, I** will become the Holy Spirit that is guiding you. No negative spirit-soul of any form will destroy your love partnership again.

From today, those who have problems in their marriages their homes and anywhere else or those who cannot love their children, those who cannot love their parents and their parents cannot love them and indeed any problem at all that you have about love, just SIGN UP FOR **THE LOVE OF THE FATHER GOD** and your problems are over. Tell **ME** that, **'FATHER GOD I LOVE YOU TOO'!** And believe it in your heart, and then you will see wonderful miraculous change in your life. And **I** will use that to forgive all your sins, because **LOVE** counts no error.

Since you answered back to **ME** and said, **I LOVE YOU TOO,** make sure your father has a copy of this. Make sure you give a copy to your mother, to your friend, your child and help everybody in this world to have a copy or access of this **SUPREME LOVE LETTER** from **THE FATHER GOD ALMIGHTY.** This is one of the Lecture Revelations that you should give to everybody

during the ***UNIVERSAL SUPREME WORD SEASON CELEBRATION.*** Give this **SUPREME LOVE LETTER** to your president, your governor, and your head of state; to your prime minister and all others and tell them **I LOVE YOU.** And let them respond **I LOVE YOU TOO.** Anybody you ask, "Do you **LOVE ME?**" If they say, "Yes **I LOVE YOU TOO.**" Say to them once more, **I LOVE YOU TOO** and give them a copy of this **SUPREME LOVE LETTER** Lecture Revelation.
If you answer **ME, 'FATHER GOD I LOVE YOU TOO'** then I will take over the situation of your life no matter how satanic you are, no matter how evil you are, even if you worship (juju) evil, but you answer **ME, I LOVE YOU TOO FATHER GOD ALMIGHTY,**

then from that moment **I** will take over your life and you become the House of God. It means you have taken a personal voluntary evolution of positive life to join with **ME THE FATHER GOD ALMIGHTY.**

If the whole world accepts this **SUPREME LOVE LETTER, then** the whole world will have **PEACE** and they will have **LOVE** because that is the power. That is where the problems came from – lack of **LOVE**. If you do not answer back to **ME,** and say *'I YOU LOVE YOU TOO'* and you are not serious about your reply to this **SUPREME UNIVERSAL FATHER GOD LOVE LETTER,** then you are in trouble. Have you ever seen **ME** before ask for Love?

This is **MY FIRST LOVE LETTER** TO ALL

HUMANKIND, to all spirits, to all souls, to all angels and for all situations. There is no more death, because if the spirit-soul of death loves **ME** it will stop being death and become life to you. If the spirit-soul of poverty in you loves **ME** and answers **I LOVE YOU TOO FATHER GOD ALMIGHTY** to **MY** declaration of **LOVE,** then the spirit-soul of poverty will become the spirit soul of riches into you. If the spirit-soul of sickness in you answers **I LOVE YOU TOO** then the spirit soul of sickness will become the spirit-soul of wellness in you. Any dire situation there is, just answer **FATHER GOD ALMIGHTY I LOVE YOU TOO**, and then **MY SPIRIT** will pierce into that situation and change it for good for you. That is the ENERGY POWER that **I** have injected in this **MY SUPREME UNIVERSAL LOVE LETTER. 'I LOVE YOU'**! And **I** mean it! **I LOVE** ALL HUMANKIND and ALL **MY** CREATIONS. They are **MY** handiwork especially human beings because they are **MY** only HOME.

Home Sweet Home! Have you not heard that said before? No matter what happens a stranger's home is not as sweet as your own home. Don't you know that it does not matter that it is said **THE FATHER GOD** lives in heaven. Where is the heaven apart from the **LOVE** of **THE FATHER GOD** for all creation? Heaven is as sweet as the **LOVE** of **GOD** is sweet with all human beings.

If **I** live in you, you sing for **ME**.
If **I** live in you, you praise **ME**.
You praise **THE FATHER GOD**.

You love another human being. It is wonderful when you do something for someone and the person says, oh thank God, Oh God bless you! It makes **ME** so happy when I hear that. You go back and kneel down and thank **THE FATHER GOD** for the good deed done for you. You say, oh **FATHER GOD THANK YOU.**

When you see someone in difficulties, if it is financial, you give the person financial assistance and the person goes to knell down and say **"FATHER GOD THANK YOU."** That is the kind of **LOVE I** want from humankind.

I established the United Kingdom as a Charity Home and that is why when there is any disaster anywhere, they would carry bags of rice and all sorts of other foods including clothing and other necessities to assist those afflicted. The Red Cross is always at hand to offer assistance. United Kingdom has helped so many souls in this world that would have been dead to life. That is why **I** blessed them. And that is why when Satan saw this he went and taught them how to go to war. Look at the United States of America: they went everywhere spreading the Word of God and doing **THE FATHER GOD'S** work. Satan went there and taught them how to go to war. Since they started engaging in wars don't you see disasters and death everywhere in those places? You must know and believe that whenever you go to war or use any other means to kill people; you have invited double of the same thing to yourself because that is the original law of karma without a reverse exception of this **SUPREME LOVE**.

No! No! No! Return to your first love that you had!
I LOVE YOU. Answer **ME** and say to **ME, "I LOVE YOU TOO FATHER GOD ALMIGHTY."** *That is what I want from the United Kingdom and the United America and the rest of the misleading countries in the world, to reply back, and say to **ME, FATHER GOD ALMIGHTY, THE CREATOR OF THE UNIVERSE, THE UNIVERSAL SUPREME WORD WE LOVE YOU TOO**.*

Now is the time that **I DEMAND THE REWARD FOR MY SHEDDING BLOOD ON THE CROSS OF CALVARY ON EARTH FOR HUMANKIND.**

NOW, **I DEMAND THE REWARD FOR MY LABOUR FOR CREATING THIS WORLD, THE WHOLE UNIVERSE AND FOR CREATING HUMAN BEINGS TO LIVE IN THEM.** That stupidity of ignoring **ME, THE FATHER GOD** your **CREATOR** has passed. If you do not answer back to **ME** with, **I LOVE YOU TOO FATHER GOD ALMIGHTY** whole heartedly in your spirit, soul and physical, thereby giving **ME** yourself to live in you, then it that means you love Lucifer and you love Satan. Therefore, where **I** put Satan and all his followers that is where **I** will put you. And **I** will DEAL with you because of being evil and you will see what will happen to you.

Any country that would not answer **ME** with, **I LOVE YOU**

TOO FATHER GOD ALMIGHTY then all the people that practice evil in that country will be destroyed. Any city that would not answer **I LOVE YOU TOO FATHER GOD ALMIGHTY** then all evil and those who practice evil will be destroyed. Give this message to your village head and your family head and everyone else.

This is how it is going to start: Husband you should tell your wife that you **LOVE THE FATHER GOD ALMIGHTY TOO,** then your wife will become an honest wife to you from that day. Wife you should tell your husband that you **LOVE THE FATHER GOD ALMIGHTY TOO** then your husband will become an honest husband to you from that day. Children should say the same thing and their parents will love them and they will also love their parents.

The family should say:
FATHER GOD ALMIGHTY I LOVE YOU TOO, then **I** will take over that family and manage it for them.

The Village Head should say:
FATHER GOD ALMIGHTY I LOVE YOU TOO, then **I** will take over that village and control it for them.

The Community Head should say:
FATHER GOD ALMIGHTY I LOVE YOU TOO, then **I** will take over that community and control it.

The Chairman of Local Government should say:
FATHER GOD ALMIGHTY I LOVE YOU TOO, then **I** will take over that Local Government and control it.

A King and Queen should say:

FATHER GOD ALMIGHTY I LOVE YOU TOO, then **I** take over their subjects and control the whole land for them.
The State should say:
FATHER GOD ALMIGHTY I LOVE YOU TOO, then **I** will take over that State and control it for them.
Those in positions of authority would be staying there as figureheads but **I THE FATHER GOD** will be doing everything for them and that is when you will see miracles. The whole country would say: **FATHER GOD ALMIGHTY I LOVE YOU TOO,** then **I** will take charge of that country and protect them.
A whole continent like Africa, Europe, America, Asia and the rest should say:
FATHER GOD ALMIGHTY I LOVE YOU TOO, then **I, THE**

SUPREME WORD OF THE UNIVERSE will be the **PEACE, LOVE** and **UNITY** that controls and manages the world that will bring salvation to all humankind.

If you are a manager and you say: **FATHER GOD ALMIGHTY I LOVE YOU TOO,** then **I** will become the manager for you. **I** will take over and do your managerial work for you. And anything at all that you need, such as a baby, if you pronounce and say:
FATHER GOD ALMIGHTY I LOVE YOU TOO, then **I** will give you a good baby. When you wish to conceive that is, before you become pregnant: say
FATHER GOD ALMIGHTY I LOVE YOU TOO, then **I** will become a child that when he or she is born, they will love you.

If you want to work and are looking for work say: **FATHER GOD ALMIGHTY I LOVE YOU TOO,** then **I** will provide a good job for you.

If you don't have money say: **FATHER GOD ALMIGHTY I LOVE YOU TOO,** then **I** will become money for you.

You can have anything that you want, provided that it is good and POSITIVE, but first of all you must sign up and say: **FATHER GOD ALMIGHTY I LOVE YOU TOO** in answer to **MY LOVE LETTER** to you.

If you reply **MY LOVE LETTER** to you in which **I** declare that **I LOVE YOU** and you answer **ME, FATHER GOD ALMIGHTY I LOVE YOU TOO,** then **MY** SWEETNESS with you starts. You know how you humans do your carnal love; **I** have **MY OWN SUPREME LOVE** which is BIGGER and more POWERFUL as **THE POSITIVE LOVE ENERGY OF LIFE. MY** nature of positive spiritual **LOVE is** based on **PEACE, MERCY, KINDNESS, EQUALITY, ONENESS** and **HONESTY** as some of **MY LOVE** instincts and sensation that will come closer to you then **I** will use the above energy of **MY LOVE** components and turn you to be positive, no matter how negative you are.

Even Lucifer, if today she says to **ME, FATHER GOD ALMIGHTY I LOVE YOU TOO,** we will make peace immediately because **I AM LOVE.** But if she refuses then **I** will continue to CAST and BAN her twenty-four hours. She is a prisoner!

I Love You, I Love You Too

Since HRM King Solomon David Jesse ETE and ETE ROYAL UNIVERSAL FAMILY said, **FATHER GOD ALMIGHTY I LOVE YOU TOO** that is why **I** *jolly-jolly* with Him now. **I** jolly with Him–o! **I** will continue to jolly with him forever.

This is open to everybody. Forget about stories. Is it stories that **I** will eat? Forget about the sentiments of human beings 'I am this and I am that.' **I** do not care about that. What **I** want is the action of your heart. **I** know those who **LOVE THE FATHER GOD** in their conscience. Do not tell **ME** or report that – oh this one did this; that one did that. That is utter rubbish! **I** know everybody's actions and your hearts.

Since **I** know that you answered **ME** back that **YOU LOVE ME** as **I LOVE YOU** then **I** will live in you and manifest **MYSELF** in you. All **MY** entourage – **MY POSITIVE SEVENTY TWO MILLION SELVES** will come and back you up and you will see the Glory of God.

Therefore, **I AM** pleading with every human soul to answer me back. Give **ME** the reply to **MY LOVE LETTER** that **I** have sent to you. **I LOVE YOU – O!** Human beings! Answer **ME** back thus:

FATHER GOD ALMIGHTY I LOVE YOU TOO.

C: **THROUGH LOVE I CREATED HUMAN BEINGS**

The reason **I** came with this Lecture Revelation today is to remind you of where we started because we started through love.

But you have been having misunderstanding all along. You have been at loggerheads. You call yourselves names, turning to things that do not exist – oh juju this, oh talisman that. Oh witchcraft this and that! Oh this! Oh that! You say, Oh I am going to protect myself with this and with that. This one says 'I am going to help you.' All that is rubbish! Due to this misunderstanding, you roamed about and started serving different spirits and different things. You left home and went wandering about.

Now! **I HAVE INVITED YOU BACK. I LOVE YOU! COME HOME! COME TO ME EVERY SOUL. COME BACK TO YOUR FATHER – YOUR FATHER GOD ALMIGHTY, YOUR CREATOR, THE**

FORCE OF YOUR LIFE, THE SUPREME WORD OF THE UNIVERSE.

Forget about church! Forget about religion. Forget about 'I am this I am that.' Forget about all that. They have no meaning. 'I am a church member. I head a religious movement. Look at me I am a Christian! Look at me I am a Muslim! Look at me I am this and look at that.' There are no meanings to all that. What has meaning now is this **OPEN LOVE LETTER - AN OPEN UNIVERSAL LOVE LETTER FROM ME THE FATHER GOD ALMIGHTY TO ALL HUMAN BEINGS. I LOVE YOU.**

You must answer **ME** back with your whole heart, with your faith, with your honest acceptance by saying to **ME: I LOVE YOU**

TOO FATHER GOD ALMIGHTY THE SUPREME WORD OF THE UNIVERSE. You must show concern, show acknowledgement and show recognition of **ME, THE SUPREME SPIRIT THE SUPREME WORD THE SUPREME SOUL IN ALL HUMAN,** then **I** will return to you as **MY** home and live in you as one entity and we will become comfortable as long as you are in **LOVE** with **ME,** your **CREATOR.**

You know, we can renew our relationship today through this invitation and your positive response. And then you will have everything back.

If you are a prodigal wife, come back.

If you are a prodigal son, come back.

Take it in your heart that TODAY! **I HAVE MADE PEACE WITH YOU.** I have forgiven you all the sins you committed, provided that you have replied positively to **MY LOVE LETTER,** and said to **ME, MY CREATOR, ALMIGHTY FATHER GOD, THE SUPREME WORD OF THE UNIVERSE,** *I LOVE YOU TOO*. Take a copy of this information and read it very well, then kneel down and knock your head on the ground, confess your sins apologizing for all the wrongs you have done to another living life like you. Confess and apologize for leaving your **FATHER GOD ALMIGHTY** to worship evil. Apologize for leaving your **FATHER GOD, THE SUPREME WORD** which is the LIFE in you, to worship something else forgetting that

THE **WORD** IS EVERYTHING for every person.
Apologize for leaving The **WORD,** your **CREATOR** whom you are supposed to thank day and night, morning and evening. You are supposed to recognize **HIM** with this reasoning that **HE** is 'the ONE that created you, **THE SUPREME BEING OF ALL THINGS, THE CREATOR OF ALL THINGS.**'
Since you did not know **ME** all this time, you missed your way and started worshipping anything. Satan captured you, misled you and put you in darkness.
Therefore, you have to come back to the **LIGHT** through this invitation of **MY UNIVERSAL SUPREME LOVE LETTER,** *I LOVE YOU.* And you must answer and say **'I LOVE YOU**

TOO FATHER GOD ALMIGHTY'.
Kneel down and knock your head on the ground. To kneel down and knock your head on the ground means, you are kneeling down and holding **MY** feet and **MY** leg and pleading by saying **FATHER GOD** forgive me! **I LOVE YOU TOO!** Immediately you say this, **FATHER GOD! FORGIVE ME! I LOVE YOU TOO! I** will enter into you from your head and send away that spirit of witchcraft in you, send away evil and barrier any negativism and baptise you in spirit, in soul and in the physical and change your environment for good!

And from that moment, you will become the rearranged house of **THE FATHER GOD!** Then the Light of **ME, THE SUPREME LIGHT OF THE UNIVERSE**

will embrace you and change that bad situation for you.
No matter how bad the situation, no matter the kind of sickness and the gravity of your illness **THE FATHER GOD ALMIGHTY** will change your situation to be good. Cancer will finish! Any type of cancer, spiritually or physically that is eating you will finish immediately you accept and reply **MY LOVE LETTER** and say **FATHER GOD ALMIGHTY, I LOVE YOU TOO**, forgive me all my transgressions! **I** will use this to cure all manners of illness and solve all manners of problems for you. And from today, miracles upon miracles and the glory of **THE FATHER GOD** has manifested on earth through this **MY OPEN LOVE LETTER** titled **I LOVE YOU** and **YOU LOVE ME TOO** to all human

beings on earth. All you need do is to answer back and say to **ME, I LOVE YOU TOO FATHER GOD ALMIGHTY.** Let the whole world say, **I LOVE YOU TOO FATHER GOD ALMIGHTY.** Let Heaven say, **I LOVE YOU TOO FATHER GOD ALMIGHTY.** Let Hades say, **I LOVE YOU TOO FATHER GOD ALMIGHTY.** Let the whole universe say, **FATHER GOD ALMIGHTY I LOVE YOU TOO,** and then there will be NO MORE destructions and NO MORE problems at all in the world. Let all principalities bow down and kneel down and knock their heads on the ground and say, **FATHER GOD ALMIGHTY I LOVE YOU TOO,** and then everything will change for good in the whole universe! However for those who refuse to act according to **MY** request, the woes will continue to visit them- the unrepented hearts.

Any continent, any country, any territory, any centre, any church, any religion, any organization, any society, any club, any individual, any soul, any spirit that refuses to give a positive response and reply to this **LOVE LETTER** from **ME, THE FATHER GOD** by NOT saying from the innersole of their heart **I LOVE YOU TOO, THE FATHER GOD ALMIGHTY,** and stop all their evil ways of life with their fellow human beings, then automatically it means that in their hearts, they are saying to **ME, THE SUPREME WORD, THE FATHER GOD ALMIGHTY**, I hate **YOU**. And the hatred that

they mean and say in their heart will return to them instantly. **You cannot keep quiet about this**. The worst thing to do is to keep quiet; every soul in all generation forever must comply for this divine order (OBEYGO). YOU MUST TAKE A STAND. YOU SHOULD NOT KEEP QUIET ABOUT THIS. YOU MUST TAKE A STAND! Immediately you come across this information –
YOU MUST TAKE A STAND. Either you accept **ME, THE FATHER GOD** and the invitation of **MY LOVE LETTER** and give a positive REPLY answer as '**I LOVE YOU TOO FATHER GOD ALMIGHTY**' or you refuse **MY LOVE LETTER TO YOU**. If you keep quiet **I** will take it that you stand for evil, and then evil will befall you.

I made humankind through **LOVE** and that is why **LOVE** is the only means that **I** will use to maintain you and put you in the **PARADISE OF THE FATHER GOD.** There is no other way.
LOVE means LIFE. LIFE means **LOVE.**
LOVE is the **SPOKEN WORD**, your **SUPREME CREATOR** and everything about all of us is **LOVE** and with that **I AM** inviting you back to **MYSELF.** You should return to your destination of **LIFE** which is **THE SUPREME WORD 'THE FATHER'S LOVE'.** And then from destination to the source of **LIFE** which is **ME THE FATHER GOD** then all is well with you.

D: LOVE IS THE ONLY WAY TO SAVE THE WHOLE WORLD

This Lecture Revelation will bring salvation to humankind. This Lecture Revelation '**MY INVITATION LOVE LETTER**' represents three things as follows; **(A), BROTHERHOOD**, Brotherhood means **I THE FATHER GOD ALMIGHTY, THE SPIRIT** of all creation put together as only ONE SUPREME UNIVERSAL FAMILY in Heaven, on Earth and in the Hades, represented by **GOD THE FATHER** in the natural physical Life of Adam THE FIRST HOUSE OF THE POSITIVE SPOKEN WORD on earth as THE UNIVERSAL GENERATION AND INCARNATION SPIRIT-SOUL.

(B), CROSS, Cross means (*FLESH*) **I THE FATHER GOD IS THE MOTHER GOD ALMIGHTY, THE SUPREME SOUL NATURE** of all creations put together as only ONE SUPREME UNIVERSAL FAMILY CHANNEL OF ALL PHYSICAL NATURES from Heaven, Earth and Hades, represented by **GOD THE SUPREME NATURE** in the natural physical Life of EVE, THE FIRST WOMB OF THE POSITIVE AND NEGATIVE SPOKEN WORD on earth as THE UNIVERSAL INCARNATION AND REINCARNATION SOUL. **(C), STAR**, Star means (**HOLY SPIRIT) LOVE, THE LIGHT OF LIFE IN HUMAN, THE HOUSE OF THE UNIVERSAL SUPREME WORD ALMIGHTY, THE CREATOR**

of all creation put together as only ONE SUPREME UNIVERSAL CONVERTER ENERGY, **THE SUPREME LIGHT, THE 'POWER' FROM THE SPIRIT SOURCE** both in Heaven, on Earth and in the Hades, represented by THE FATHER SON AND HOLY SPIRIT AS THE TRINITY to manifest THE TOTALITY of LOVE BETWEEN THE FATHER AND MOTHER GOD, SPIRITUAL AND NATURAL POWER OF THE SUPREME WORD by a natural and Spiritual Personified WORD AS THE CHRIST, THE KING OF KINGS AND THE LORD OF LORDS, THE HEAD OF THE HUMAN GOD AND THE HOLY SPIRIT OF TRUTH, THE SOLE SPIRITUAL HEAD LIVING IN EVERY HEART, LOVE, LOVE AND LOVE, THE TOTAL

GLORY of **THE FATHER GOD,** the last personified **SUPREME WORD** in the last incarnate **ADAM** and **EVE, OLUMBA** and **OBU,** the same first universal Brotherhood in the Garden, and **I THE FATHER GOD** in Adam was THE KING OF KINGS, THE FIRST HUMAN GOD, THE FATHER ON EARTH. The second universal Brotherhood was when I THE FATHER GOD visited the world as THE TOTAL SUPREME WORD in **OUR LORD JESUS CHRIST** to reunite **MY SUPREME FAMILY** the Universal Brotherhood with **MY DIVINE LOVE** on the Cross of Calvary Tree.

Brotherhood, Cross and Star is the total and complete manifestation of **MY** business here on earth.

The Tree of the Calvary cross was the symbol of **LOVE** for all **MY** creation; **BROTHERHOOD** itself is total LOVE, but the meaning of CROSS and STAR are LIFE or DEATH in that if you accept **MY INVITATION** to carry the cross of **LOVE ONE and ANOTHER,** *then you shall live forever with ME in spirit, soul and physical, but if you denial MY LAST INVITATION OF LOVE, it means that you have refused to carry the cross of LOVE to LIFE, then you shall perish and your blood shall be upon your head.* **I, THE FATHER GOD** do not wish that your soul should perish because **I LOVE YOU; I AM** your universal spiritual **FATHER** in **BROTHERHOOD** of the universal Parenthood.

The CROSS means the acceptance of this **SUPREME LOVE INVITATION** to **LOVE** everyone wherever you are. **I AM** not interested in a religion or any other type of organisation. What **I** want from all human beings on earth is to live in **LOVE, PEACE** and **UNITY.** When you accept the **LOVE** in this **LOVE LETTER,** which is the Spiritual Calvary Tree of Christ, the OPEN INVITATION, as **I** say to you, **I LOVE YOU** and you accept **ME, THE SUPREME WORD** and reply to **ME** with full believe, SAYING **I LOVE YOU TOO. ....Then all is well with you** This is the same pronouncement that **I** made more than two thousand years ago that **I LOVE YOU,** and then **I** exercised these words on the cross, by dying naked for humankind. **I** finished that assignment. Now, **I** require reciprocal action - WORK FOR **ME I** WORK FOR YOU!

Because **I** died on the cross for humankind in the first place to show **MY LOVE** for humanity, this is the time that everyone must deny his or her negativisms. Deny all your evil ways of life and work for **THE FATHER GOD** by loving your follow human being as **I LOVE YOU.** If you refuse this order, you will never resurrect with **ME,** and you will not escape damnation.

To save your life means to save the whole world and that is by you replying this letter with faith: **I LOVE YOU TOO FATHER GOD ALMIGHTY** with a total repented heart from all practical evil and hatred you committed against a follow human being like you.

I WANT THIS INFORMATION TO BE PREPARED AS SOON AS POSSIBLE. **I AM** EXPECTING THIS INFORMATION TO BE OUT WITHIN THE NEXT THREE TO FOUR WEEKS TO COINCIDE WITH ***THE UNIVERSAL SUPREME WORD SEASON CELEBRATION.*** THIS LETTER IS TO BE USED TO OPEN THE WEEK therefore I want this Lecture Revelation to come out as a book – a proper book that the whole world would have a copy. A proper book that every individual in the whole wide world would have a copy to answer **MY LOVE LETTER** and say to **ME: I LOVE YOU TOO FATHER GOD ALMIGHTY. I** KNOW THAT PRINCESS MFON ETTEH, HRM QUEEN DISEM SOLOMON DAVID

JESSE ETE AND HRM KING SOLOMON DAVID JESSE ETE and the rest of the human beings will promote this universal information. They must circulate **MY LOVE LETTER TO THE WHOLE UNIVERSE,** so that **I** will solve all humanities problems, in the Name and the Blood of Our Lord Jesus Christ. Amen!

Yes! Through **LOVE I** made human beings and **I** live in you. Through **LOVE I** made everything therefore all human beings have to reciprocate this **LOVE OF THE FATHER GOD** since **LOVE IS EVERYTHING ON EARTH. LOVE** is the only means to save this world. With **LOVE** the world shall be saved because **I** died for humankind to save the world. It is hatred that destroyed the world. All of

Nigeria, Ghana and African Countries and United Kingdom, European Countries, United America and Asia, Russia, Iraq, Iran, all the Philistines, all the Arab world, all Christendom, all Muslims, all religions, as a matter of fact everybody, no matter who or what you are, as long as you are a human being you must answer and reply **ME** the **LOVE LETTER that have I** written to you with '**I LOVE YOU TOO FATHER GOD ALMIGHTY**'. If you do, then we will be in peace with all Brotherhood of LOVE ONE and ANOTHER, which means that we are of one Family of the same Father and Mother therefore there should be no more wars and hatred in the whole world.

Those who are fighting should drop their weapons now by loving

THE FATHER GOD. They should CEASE FIRE! This letter is called CEASE FIRE of all negativism and of all hatred and **WARS**, because **THE SUPREME WORD OF THE UNIVERSE** has invited you for **LOVE.** And you **MUST** accept this **POSITIVE PRACTICAL LOVE MOVEMENT.** If you deny then the war is no more with human beings rather you are at war with your **CREATOR, THE SUPREME WORD OF THE UNIVERSE** as your life therefore, it will become your personal and internal war with your soul, **THE ONE** that created you. This means that you have declared yourself a warrior, fighting against **THE FATHER GOD ALMIGHTY.** That is what it means to deny **THE FATHER**

GOD'S SUPREME PEACE AND LOVE.
However if you accept **ME, THE FATHER GOD ALMIGHTY'S LOVE** and answer **I LOVE YOU TOO FATHER GOD ALMIGHTY,** then all is well with you and the whole world. This is the only way that the world will be saved in the name and blood of Our Lord Jesus Christ, Amen.

E: **THOSE WHO LOVE SHALL BE SAVED**

If you accept this **LOVE** that **I, THE FATHER GOD ALMIGHTY AM** extending to you, then, you are automatically saved. If you believe this **WORD** and appreciate with **ME THE SUPREME WORD OF THE UNIVERSE,** you are automatically saved, just as those who call Jesus! Jesus! Jesus! They shout Jesus Christ on the Calvary Tree, Jesus Christ on the cross, Jesus of Nazareth, The Blood of Christ! This is much more than that. This is the LIFE of JESUS CHRIST!

DO NOT CALL THE BLOOD of JESUS CHRIST alone, but also call on THE LIFE OF JESUS CHRIST, which is **LOVE YE ONE ANOTHER.**

From today, the Supreme Power, the Supreme Energy that is inside **LOVE**, which is **THE FATHER GOD ALMIGHTY** is **CHRIST HIMSELF.** And **LOVE HIMSELF** will activate in anybody that replies **I LOVE YOU TOO FATHER GOD ALMIGHTY.**

This is not the love of fornication. This is not a kind of LOVE that if you tell a man or woman that you love him or her immediately they starting thinking about sexuality and turn it into counterfeit and carnal love for evil use.

Today, **MY LOVE LETTER** to all creations is the invitation for **EVERLASTING LIFE**. It is no more theory. It is **PRACTICAL LOVE.** It is by demonstration, by instinct, by character, by peace, by equality, by oneness, by mercy and by all quantities of good characters. That is **I LOVE YOU TOO,** because **I,** the **WORD** live in all Christians.

The same **WORD** lives in all Muslims.

The same **WORD** lives in all Jews.

The same **WORD** lives in everyone as a man or woman, a child or an adult. The same **WORD** lives in all human beings in the whole wide world. Everybody breathes the same air, so, if you say **I LOVE YOU TOO,** it means you will not hate any human being again from that second. This is the only communion that **ME,** and you are going to make - The DIVINE UNION OF **THE FATHER GOD ALMIGHTY** with HUMANKIND. If I say **I LOVE YOU.** You say **I LOVE YOU TOO.** When you answer like that, then you have communion with **ME, THE FATHER GOD ALMIGHTY.** We have entered into union of ONE LOVE, ONE UNITY, ONE PEACE, ONE JOY and that is joy, joy, joy, everywhere, here and there! Do not tell **ME** lies! Do not play the fool with **ME, THE FATHER GOD.** DO NOT TELL ME LIES.

I Love You, I Love You Too

If you do, you are going to be in BIG trouble.

Since you have declared that **YOU LOVE ME TOO,** do not play **ME** *mago-mago (tricks)*. Do not hate **ME** any more! We are now doing everything together.

Just accept and say **I LOVE YOU TOO.** Promote this **WORD.** Sign up for this **GOODWILL LOVE** of **THE FATHER GOD ALMIGHTY** then **I** and all **MY** positive selves and all good things will find our way to where you are.

People struggle too much in Africa. Some people in deprived countries in the world make efforts to go to the Western World. Many Nigerians and Ghanaians, Zimbabweans as well as others go to live in the United Kingdom, for instance. Many African people are all over

European countries, United States of America and other parts of the Western World. Why?
It is not as if these places are very nice. United Kingdom for instance is very cold in the winter season and in other places the cold is quite intolerable but you know what? The Europeans and other people of the Western World make their countries nice to attract people. They make life comfortable. Electricity supply is constant, so also is gas supply and good roads and transports. There is constant availability of clean water right inside your house. They really establish a good quality of physical life and make great efforts to make life comfortable in their countries and this attracts others to leave their home and country to go and live and work for them. And they

make sure you pay for it. When you work they divide the money into two and take one part. That is the type of thing you should be doing if you love yourself.
If you **LOVE YOURSELF** why you don't do like that in your country for everyone to happy.
Why can Nigerians not do like that in their country?
Why can Ghanaians not do like that in their country?
Why can the rest of Africans not do like that in their countries?
Why is it that the United Kingdom and the United States of America and others not help other less privilege countries in the world? If you make living comfortable in your countries the light-skin humans that is, those in the Western World will come and live in your country. It will attract them to live there. These sets of

people do not mind making anywhere in the world their home as long as the place is comfortable.

You see, the light-skin humans are very advanced in character. The Light-skin humans as the group of people you humans call Whiteman are no longer living in the jungle as far as physical living is concerned. They have gone too far in the physical life. They do not believe that they come from anywhere. They believe that wherever life is comfortable that is their home. That is **THE FATHER GOD'S LOVE** in nature. But you see Africans they are still *chughu-chughu-chughu* in character. They are yet to discern themselves.

You Africans and others from other physically undeveloped places would not stay where you are and make your home comfortable. Why do you run to go to Europe and to the other Western Worlds? You go to Western world to live and those from the Western Worlds go to your place to carry your oil and other minerals back to their country and then sell it back to you, because you do not have **LOVE AND UNDERSTANDING** of your self. Riches without understanding and **PERFECT LOVE OF ONE ANOTHER**, have no benefits, and have no meaning to the human true nature and with **ME** your **CREATOR**.

From today! Say: **I LOVE YOU TOO FATHER GOD ALMIGHTY.** Then you will see the goodness of **THE FATHER GOD.** All scientists, technologists, prominent people and all

knowledgeable people should use what they have to make life equal for everyone. This means that as you build good roads in Europe, America, China and the Arabs, you must also build good roads, good things that make life comfortable in African countries and other places in the world. If your life is good make life good for everybody and that means you **LOVE THE FATHER GOD. I LOVE YOU TOO** does not only mean **YOU LOVE ME THE FATHER GOD** in theory. It means you **LOVE** to share what you have with others, which mean you love yourself too.
When **I** say, **I LOVE YOU** and you answer **I LOVE YOU TOO** that means you love yourself back. If you do not answer like that in practical love, it means in reality you hate yourself, because you do

not know where your next place of birth of your next visit on earth will be.

You see, let **ME** use HRM King Solomon David Jesse ETE as an example of what happens in life. HRM King Solomon David Jesse ETE's last visit on earth was in Europe as King James the 1st of England, but now He is from a remote village in Nigeria called Ikot Okwo in Ikot Abasi Local Government area of Akwa Ibom State.

When **I** say the place is remote, it is a real BUSH. **I** mean there is no road. Well, it is now that they are trying to create some sort of roads there. There is no electricity. What would you call such a situation? Would you say it is a blessing? Or would you say it is punishment? He came back like that for a reason. The same thing obtains

you who siphon things from there to here and here to there. That place from which you removed those good things, **I** will send you to that place on your next birth on earth. And the people that you took that precious thing from **I** will send them to born where you took those things to. That is **MY** program, because **I AM** a **TRUTHFUL** Judge.
Are you a **WORD?**
Are you a **LIFE?**
Do you know **MY** Central Administration Office in spirit?
Do you know where they process people for birth and rebirth?
Are you from there?
Do you have a clue where you come from?
You do not even know yourself and do not know your real spiritual name?

If **I, THE FATHER GOD** did not reveal to HRM King Solomon ETE who He is, from him as Abel the brother of Cain, He would not know Himself.

ALL SECRETS ARE IN **MY** HAND. You better say **I LOVE YOU TOO** and that means you are saved.

Since **I LOVE** humankind being **MY** home and as **MYSELF** – '**I AND MY FATHER ARE ONE.**' This means that humankind and **I** are **ONE**. How could **I** therefore, hate any human being that **I** have created?

The behaviour of human-animals made **ME** to always destroy humankind. However, now **I** want **LOVE** to reign. With understanding and peace everywhere, **I** will silence cyclone, **I** will silence hurricane and **I** will silence earthquake and all natural disasters. **I** will silence everything that raises its head on you but if you refuse to comply with **MY** Ordinance of **LOVE** you will see what will happen to you.

F: **YOU ARE CONDEMNED UNLESS YOU LOVE**

If you do not **LOVE** and you throw this **LOVE LETTER** away and you do not care, your not caring, attitude means you condemn yourself. There is no need to talk too much about this. Instead, you should accept the invitation and respond positively well, believe and surrender yourself and accept the instructions of **THE FATHER GOD.** Take the Test of the Universal Brotherhood of **THE FATHER GOD,** which is *THE*

UNIVERSAL SUPREME WORD SEASON CELEBRATION.

Donate heavily for the celebration according to your capacity. Share what you have with happiness and joy. Sign unto the program properly and without questioning the authority of it.

Governments of all countries must sign on to this program of **THE UNIVERSAL THE SUPREME WORD SEASON CELEBRATION** <u>and to know how the funds utilise in a way and manner that</u> **I THE FATHER GOD** <u>permitted universally</u>. There is NO COUNTRY that is bigger than this celebration of **SUPREME WORD**. United States of America should be involved and donate for the **UNIVERSAL CELEBRATION** to help all humanity. United Kingdom should be involved and

donate to the program. All countries of the world, every individual, all families should be officially involved with ***THE UNIVERSAL SUPREME WORD SEASON CELEBRATION.***
Everything must be recorded.
Do not go to spoil this program in any way.
Do not bring any high-sense to it.
Do not bring academia and your academic knowledge in a negative way in it; rather use your knowledge and position to help this program in a positive manner.
Do not bring anything in an attempt to override **MY UNIVERSAL SUPREME PROGRAM.**
You should rather follow the given instructions to the letter. No human being should give directives regarding ***THE UNIVERSAL CELEBRATION***

OF THE SUPREME WORD except the one who is the Head of this program. Abel the second Son of **GOD THE FATHER** the 1st ADAM is the person who initiated this program in the beginning of time. He has the template for the program. He has the seal, so, please keep all your carnal and negative knowledge aside and join Him for this celebration. Then you shall see immediate change and blessing on earth.

G: **LOVE IS THE ONLY REMEDY**

LOVE is **THE ONLY REMEDY** because without of **LOVE** humankind would not be created in the first place. **I** said – LET **US** MAKE MAN IN OUR OWN IMAGE AND LIKENESS. **I** spoke to **MYSELF** and all the creations that existed spiritually then, **I BUILT MAN WITH MY OWN HANDS**, and man was not developed.

I created man with **MY OWN** hands in **MY IMAGE** and **LIKENESS** not the case of development of humans as some people theorize that man developed from animal species. Nevertheless, there are human beings that came from other species. They are the evolutional humans from animals. They cause lots of trouble. They are the people that go to war, kill their fellow human beings and commit all sort evil atrocities. The real human being that **I** created with **MY OWN** hands and lived in, was the spirit called Adam. He is **GOD THE FATHER** on Earth. **GOD THE FATHER** was Adam, the first human **GOD** on earth.

The 1st **KING** and He manifested that kingship through when he was **KING DAVID** because King David was the same natural Adam in nature.
The **WORD** lived in Him.
That **WORD** is called **GOD**.
Then **THE FATHER GOD** is **THE SPIRIT** that produced the **WORD.** That **SPIRIT** is what is known as **THE FATHER GOD ALMIGHTY.** The **WORD** is the **ONE** that revealed the two of them. The **WORD** revealed **THE FATHER GOD** and revealed **GOD THE FATHER.** That is the **OOO** in you that you do not understand. When you hear **OOO** you think it is juju, you think is demon or Satan.
OOO – **OLUMBA OLUMBA OBU** - **I** came to establish that entity name as **LEADER OLUMBA OLUMBA OBU.**

LEADER means the FOUNDER, the DIRECTOR. FATHER means the OWNER. **THE FATHER** is the spiritual part of **ME.** And **THE LEADER** is the physical **ONE** directing. **OOO** is the **SUPREME WORD – THE SUPREME WORD OF THE UNIVERSE** the **ONE** talking now. Whether you believe it or not it is **THE TRUTH.**

Do you know the meaning of Adam and the name **OLUMBA OLUMBA OBU?**

OBU means **DUST** in Efik and Ibibio language - Dust of the Universe. Every human being is dust.

The first **OLUMBA** means the **SPIRIT.**

The second **OLUMBA** means the **SOUL.**

SPIRIT and SOUL inside DUST, that is **OLUMBA OLUMBA**

OBU who is the KING of Kings and the LORD of Lords, the **SUPREME WORD OF THE UNIVERSE.** That is it.
If you sign up and say:
I LOVE YOU TOO FATHER GOD ALMIGHTY then, all your problems are solved for eternity.

If any spirit in you hindered you and you do not accept this Truth, well your end shall tell you. But it might be too late for you to do anything. This is the only remedy for all humankind's problems. **I LOVE YOU. I** need a reply, and it should be, **I LOVE YOU TOO** in spirit, soul and physical.

CONCLUSION A:
NOBODY CAN BYPASS LOVE

Because **I THE HOLY SPIRIT OF TRUTH** is **LOVE** you cannot bypass **ME.** If you try to bypass **ME** you are deceiving yourself. No human being can bypass **LOVE** in anything. You say you love your wife, but you bypass that **LOVE** and live in pretence, hence, your marriage does not work. The wife says she loves her husband, but would bypass that **LOVE** and that is when the marriage would not work. The children also bypass **LOVE**. The same thing occurs with any relationship whether at your workplace, government or at home. When you bypass the original **LOVE** of **THE FATHER GOD** in that place, in

that person, then that connection in the relationship will not work. This means that there is no way you can bypass **ME THE SUPREME LOVE.**
LOVE is the Leader.
LOVE is the Gateman.
LOVE is everything.
LOVE is the **SUPREME WORD.**
LOVE is the only singular that became plural and that is **THE LEADER.** It is the **HOLY SPIRIT OF TRUTH.** It is **THE FATHER GOD;** therefore, you cannot bypass **ME, THE FATHER GOD ALMIGHTY** for any reason.

CONCLUSION B:
THIS IS HUMANITY'S LAST CHANCE

This is humanity's last chance. **I, THE SUPREME LOVE** carried the cross of sins to restore humanity to **MYSELF**. Now you must carry the cross of *LOVE ONE AND ANOTHER*. To accept **THE LOVE** of **THE FATHER GOD** is to save your soul and the world.

I speak in an understandable way and **I** know that Princess Mfon Etteh is going to transcribe this Lecture Revelation very well and then give to HRM King Solomon David Jesse ETE and Queen Disem Solomon ETE to finalize it, and publish it immediately. This book should come out as a Letter in *THE UNIVERSAL*

SUPREME WORD SEASON CELEBRATION.
This is the only last chance that **I AM** giving to human beings through this invitation of **LOVE** that **I AM** extending to all humankind and you must accept. **I LOVE YOU.** You must give **ME** a reply with full acceptance and say:
I LOVE YOU TOO FATHER GOD ALMIGHTY, THE SUPREME WORD OF THE UNIVERSE.
Thereafter you join **MY** Principal Directives, which includes, **LOVE YE ONE ANOTHER**, be a peacemaker, be kind, be in oneness, be merciful and practice righteousness. There must be NO wars, no suppression, no tribalism, segregation and division.
In the Supreme Future everything is oneness and

everything is **LOVE** in the whole universe.

There shall be one passport for everybody. The Universal Supreme Passport of **THE FATHER GOD** is **LOVE**. For those who have **LOVE, I** will give them a Spiritual Passport and they will use that to penetrate everywhere with authority. **I** will put a seal on the Spiritual Passport that means you are free everywhere and wherever you go. As a result, you can go to Hades and come back.

You can go to Heaven and come back.

Nobody will have any right on you except **THE FATHER GOD.** That is the passport that **I** will give to all the people that accepts this **LOVE** today, in the name and blood of Our Lord Jesus Christ. It is a passport to pass any situation including death and any other situation. And **THE FATHER GOD** will come and go in you. This is the LAST CHANCE THAT **I** GIVE TO HUMANKIND. If you accept **MY LOVE** then you are free.

CONCLUSION C:

I LOVE YOU

I conclude this **SUPREME INVITATION LOVE LETTER** with **I LOVE YOU** and **I** want your reply. Fishes, birds, animals, trees, grasses, plants, air, spirit, soul, human beings and everything as the totality of everything. You must give **ME** a reply of this letter. **I** want to receive the reply of **MY LOVE LETTER** to you as soon as possible from all creations. It is only evil and negative human beings, people with hatred nature, demons and all satanic people that will not like this information because they do not want to change to the good part of **THE FATHER GOD,** but if they accept **MY SUPREME DIVINE** invitation of **LOVE** and reply to **ME** and say, **I LOVE YOU TOO FATHER GOD ALMIGHTY,** then all is well with **ME** and them.

This **LOVE LETTER** that **I AM** sending to all humankind is the last chance. It is the last remedy for all. Human beings have forgotten **MY** relationship with them but **MY** relationship with you will be renewed when you give **ME** the reply to this letter.

Let **my** peace and blessing abide with the entire world, now and forever more. Amen.
THANK YOU FATHER

I Love You, I Love You Too

Chapter Two

FATHER'S TALK
(GOD PRESENT)

Christ Our Lord, Thirteenth Bartholomew, FATHER,
Two Thousand and Eight (AC/OI/BOOH)
Saturday, Thirteenth September, Year Two Thousand and
Eight (13/09/2008)

In the Name of Our Lord Jesus Christ, In the Blood our Jesus Christ, Now and forever More Amien

THE UNIVERSAL UPDATE

===============

WARNING! BY THE FATHER GOD ALMIGHTY

Today, it pleases **ME, THE FATHER GOD** to give this Lecture Revelation titled **THE UNIVERSAL UPDATE: WARNING! BY THE FATHER GOD ALMIGHTY.**

INTRODUCTION

NOT THIS TIME AROUND!

Not This Time Around is the **Introduction** title of this Lecture Revelation. **I AM** bringing this INFORMATION out from The RECORDS of **MY** INNER SELF because *eboh! ama oyem ndimia ntre utong eyen afo wut enye ikpa* - if you want to cane a stubborn child first show him or her the cane.
I AM UPDATING THE WHOLE UNIVERSE today. Maybe they have forgotten the

stories about **THE FATHER GOD.** Maybe they have forgotten all the information **I** gave at various times since the creation to the present. From time to time **I** have been **UPDATING THE WHOLE UNIVERSE.** The entire **FATHER GOD'S TALK (GOD PRESENT)** in the Bible from GENESIS to REVELATION, THE EVERLASTING GOSPELS, And **THE FATHER'S TALK (GOD PRESENT)** Lecture Revelations and all the preaching from preachers that **I** have inspired in the whole universe are all **UPDATES.**

Today! This is **A UNIVERSAL SUPREME UPDATE FROM THE FATHER GOD ALMIGHTY DIRECT TO ALL MY CHILDREN,** to all creations, to all humankind, so that you will know that this thing that you take so easy-easy is not easy-o-o! What is going to befall the stubborn children will not be easy for them. You are not going to find what will befall you easy to bear.

I AM LOVE.
I AM PATIENCE.
I AM MERCY.
I have talked and talked and talked and shouted. I warned and warned and warned! I give all sorts of warnings that human beings should stop wickedness, should stop fighting, should stop quarrelling, should stop killing, should stop all the evil things they do and live in love and peace but it seems that humankind does not want to listen.

What happened in the time of Noah?

What happened to Sodom and Gomorrah?

What happened to Babylon?

What happened to Pharaoh and all the other people that were stubborn against the VOICE OF GOD?

Go back to history. If you do not believe history check around the family you come from, check around people and check everything else in your vicinity and all around the world and you find that things always happen contrary to expectations, even with confirmed predictions. Nonetheless, of all the disasters, plaques and other incidents that has happened at previous times since creation, this is going to be the worst, if that is what you want. This is the most endurable period for all **THE FATHER GOD'S** children.

This **UPDATE** is for both **POSITIVE** and negative people. If you are on **THE FATHER**

GOD'S side and you listen to **THE FATHER GOD** and believe **THE FATHER GOD** then you can do something to end the problems or you can leave the problems to continue.

There is no way that any human being, spirit, soul, or creation can continue to think that **I THE FATHER GOD THE CREATOR OF THE UNIVERSE, THE SUPREME WORD, THE OWNER, THE CREATOR** would allow the children of God to continue to suffer, crying, weeping and gnashing their teeth and **I** would allow wickedness to continue to flourish on earth freely as it is going on now. Those who practice evil or those who come from evil, support and promote the evil ones and evil activities know what **I** mean by evil. They know what wickedness is. They deprive people things they should have. The evil ones are those who are wicked to people, those who kill people, those who suppress people and allow others to lament. What is the meaning of the evil things you do? All of you who do these things know what **I AM** talking about. If you think your evil practices, your acts of wickedness and your destructions are the works of **THE FATHER GOD ALMIGHTY, I** will prove to you that they are not. They are the works of evil and **I** will give you that cup once and for all because: When you kill off those who kill, then there will be no more killing. When you destroy death then, there will be no more death. When you destroy evil then there will be no more evil.

When you destroy those who practice wickedness then there would be no more wickedness. For this reason, **I AM NOW GIVING UPDATES** for everyone to know that he or she will still receive the cup of their deeds from the tide of *THE UNIVERSAL GREAT CHANGE*.

This is **AN UPDATE** to *THE UNIVERSAL GREAT CHANGE* for you to know that the wicked people, the evil people in this world will not get away with their wickedness and evils. **I AM** addressing the situation via disasters and other various problems. In essence what **I AM** saying is that **MY** feet and every part of **ME** are on the earth turning around and around and around every second. And when **I** turn to reach anything that does not bring Glory to **THE FATHER GOD, I** will destroy it. The world will not end the way you think. It will not disappear the way you think but all evil and the practicing of evil will end, whether you believe it or not. That is the **UNIVERSAL UPDATE** and also the introduction of **Not This Time Around** that people would use means to destroy things and destroy people.

Rather there are more and more children of **GOD** and more positive children of **THE FATHER GOD** on earth. The Blood of Christ has salvaged so many souls for **HIMSELF** for **THE FATHER GOD.** For this reason **I AM** using this opportunity to announce that those who practice '**LOVE ONE ANOTHER**,' as those who listen to **THE FATHER GOD** and believe **THE FATHER GOD** will see the Glory of GOD.

If you say you did not have the opportunity to believe our first Father on earth who was Adam as God the Father on earth, and you did not have the opportunity to believe all the prophets even Our Lord Jesus Christ who came on earth because you claim that you did not see **HIM** and know **therefore you do** not believe them and dismissed their information as just stories: then what about **THE HOLY SPIRIT OF TRUTH THE FATHER GOD ALMIGHTY,** NOW ON EARTH PHYSICALLY, THE **ONE** TALKING NOW, THE DIVINE SPIRIT? **I AM TALKING NOW!**

I AM THE FATHER GOD ALMIGHTY talking now through that DIVINE SPIRIT of

THE HOLY SPIRIT OF TRUTH. So, you have the opportunity NOW to listen to **THE HOLY SPIRIT**. And the WORD of **THE HOLY SPIRIT** is LOVE ONE ANOTHER. You should be in spirit with one another.
You should practice equality with one another.
You should practice mercy with one another.
You should practice kindness.
You should practice righteousness.
You should make things to be easy with everyone.
You must not stand on people's way.
And you should not suppress anyone.

If you are a head of a country, do not bring disaster to your people. **I AM** now telling the whole world that what you are going to see is because of what you do if you did not know that already.

A: I AM THE UNIVERSAL UPDATE

I AM THE SUPREME WORD OF THE UNIVERSE. I AM THE UPDATE MYSELF.
Every EVENT is **I THE SUPREME WORD.**
Every PROGRAM is **I THE SUPREME WORD**
Every THOUGHT is **I THE SUPREME WORD**
When you plan evil do not believe that as you are planning your evil, **THE FATHER GOD** does not know your evil plan. You cannot bypass **ME** to do anything and you know what happens when you miss the track. The correct track for every human being on earth to walk on is what **I AM** now coming to provide, through **THE**

FATHER'S TALK (GOD PRESENT), THE EVERLASTING GOSPEL and all other directives from **THE FATHER GOD ALMIGHTY.** All the information within the above channels is to help you walk in the track of **THE FATHER GOD.** Our Lord Jesus Christ who is incarnate Adam has informed the whole world that since the Natural Father made a mistake, the Spiritual Father who is also known as the Son of Man came and corrected that situation therefore, 'I AND MY FATHER ARE ONE' applies to all children of GOD that practice **LOVE YE ONE** Another. No human being should kill another human being. 'Thou shalt not kill'. No human being should think evil or plan evil or any form of wickedness whether in spirit, in soul or physical against another person. Your manner of living should be with the principle of, Live and Let Live. All you should do as one that has life is to always try to help people in a positive way, particularly those who cannot help themselves. You should not invite any spirit- soul or physical entity of any kind to back you to do evil. In truth, it is better that you throw yourself into the deep sea than engage with any spirit-soul to back you to do evil. It is better you attach a heavy stone, more than one hundred kilograms in weight to a rope and tie it around your neck and throw yourself into the ocean and bury yourself there, than for you to be a witch or wizard and hurt or harm people with witchcraft or in any other form or to wish people evil and to

do all sorts of evil that you know about. If you know consciously that you are doing evil and you do not pray over it and make any purposeful or deliberate effort to stop, you will be sorry for yourself for what will befall you.
I AM THE UNIVERSAL UPDATE! AND I AM UPDATING EVERY SOUL NOW! The only way out so that peace can reign in the world so that there will be peace in the family, peace in your personal life, peace in any government, peace in any situation, peace in any level of life is for you to take this **UPDATE** and stop practising evil. Stop all the programs you have which you know is evil right away! All governments in this world should stop all evil programs. All groups of people, as kings, queens, head of states,

presidents, a man, a woman, a child, an adult, spirits, angels, souls or whatever else you are or you stand for, stop practicing negativism! Voluntarily stop your negative practices. Do not wait until **I** stop you by force because if **I** stop you by force, that is war and it means destruction.
Nonetheless, if you stop voluntarily from today as you hear this information and you hands off all negative life and stop all the wickedness of your life such as partiality, arrogance and hypocrisy as well as tribalism and run to life, run to peace, run to love, and embrace peace, embrace love and love one another and be peaceful, you become easy to be entreated, then you are safe from destruction. You should believe that you come from one Father and one Mother, which is **THE FATHER GOD**

that manifested Adam on earth. Every human being is one brother and one sister. If you know this and stop evil, then you sign up for **THE FATHER GOD** to rescue the situation for you. If you do not stop your wickedness, then you prove yourself to be evil. And the Holy Spirit has come to destroy all evils.

The voice you are hearing talking now is not the voice of a human being. Human beings cannot talk. Nobody can talk without **THE FATHER GOD** in that person talking. You have two channels. One channel is positive and the other is negative. The **POSITIVE** channel is the one **I AM** talking through for the Glorification of **THE FATHER GOD** and for easy and peaceful life on earth. The negative channel is the one that you are using to talk evil. It is the channel you use to kick against this VOICE. That negative channel! **I AM** going to close it down for eternity! When **I** close that studio down for life, then you will be no more to be found. This is **AN UPDATE. I AM THE UNIVERSAL UPDATE.**

B: **WHAT IS GOING ON IN YOUR MIND**

I AM UPDATING YOU on what is on your mind. As you are hearing this **WORD** or reading this **WORD**– whichever applies, two things are going on in your mind.
One:
Should I repent?
Should I listen to this WORD?
Should I take this WORD seriously?
Who is talking now?

Since that is what is going on in your mind, **I** want to tell you that the **WORD** you are hearing, the universal update information you are hearing and the program **I** have at hand now is to prove the true children of **GOD** and you should stop all that thinking and join **MY** program. Stop immediately if you are negative and be positive! **I say,** if you repent you stand a chance to save your life.

The whole world is shaking! ***THE GREAT UNIVERSAL CHANGE*** is at work. **I AM THE GREAT UNIVERSAL CHANGE** shaking the whole world. If there is any instrument that you think you can create, go ahead and create it. Anything you think you can do to barrier **ME,** try it. **I AM** aware of everything that is going on in human hearts. **I AM** going to shake the evil until the last evil falls before **I** leave this world in peace. **I AM** going to shake every corner so that wherever they bury any evil **I** will bring it out. If you tie any evil around your waist, **I** shake you and shake you until it falls off your waist. Any country that worships dragon and have left the **TRUE GOD, THE SUPREME FATHER GOD,** the **ONE** that created them to worship the creation, **I** will shake them until their eyes open.

Those who promote negativity and carnality and create energy for evil – for Satan to fight against **ME, I** will shake them until **I** render them useless down to zero. **THIS IS AN UPDATE.**

You know in your mind what you are thinking has nothing to do with this WORD. Nevertheless, **I** want you to know this. You send a

message with the WORD to a friend to come and see you. Your friend hears the message via the WORD and comes to see you. You order your workers to go and do some work so that you would pay them. They obey your order because you are the big person or because you are the director or the manager. You use the WORD to give instructions to your children, your wife, your friend and they use love to listen to you. You invite people for any occasion and they come. You are the head of secret society or the head of church or a president of a country or a king or a queen, you give orders and your subjects' honour you. They honour you because they kept you where you are.
A president, a governor, a village head, a king, a queen gives orders and people follow the order. As a

matter of fact every head and every senior gives orders with the WORD to their subjects and they hear the WORD and obey but who is your senior? **WHO IS THE ALL AND ALL HEAD? THE FATHER GOD, THE SUPREME WORD OF THE UNIVERSE** is the **ONE**.

I AM GIVING YOU THE ORDER! THIS IS NOW THE VOICE YOU MUST OBEY. You should obey this **WORD** of **THE FATHER'S TALK (GOD PRESENT)** Lecture Revelations. **THEY ARE THE WORDS OF THE FATHER GOD ALMIGHTY.**

I pass through people to preach on televisions but you ignore them.
They preach in newspapers and you ignore.
They preach everywhere yet you continue to ignore.

You go to church and other religious centres but you do not practice the good teaching that is preached there. You preach good things but you not practice what you preach.

Those who call themselves governments of this world are the worst. The general notion seems to be that if you are a President, Head of State, Prime Minister, Governor or you occupy important governmental post then you should not worship **THE FATHER GOD.** Who is supposed to know **THE FATHER GOD** more? Government means **GOD'S** Common Purse for everybody but the government of today believe that they have nothing to do with **THE FATHER GOD.** If you are this type of person, then prepare yourself for where you will find yourself.

Now, **THE UPDATE** is this. It can be because of one evil person that disaster comes to where you live so if you are a good person and you hear this message, say **'FATHER GOD!** I will not share with the evil ones.' You are working in the office of the president, with the head of state, with the governor, your father, your mother, your relations or anyone else that you may be working with and you know that they are doing evil, do not support such a person no matter what it will cost you. Tell the person that you do not support their evil work because if you keep quiet what will befall that person that is doing that evil will befall you too. If you hear that someone plans to kill and you keep quiet and the person goes and kills, then you and that person are together in that crime. If you hear of any evil that someone is planning to execute and you do not expose that person to exclude yourself, you would be judged with that person because you are a witness to the crime. If someone plans to go to war with another person or group to go and bully them and you are in support then what befalls that person will befall you too.

I, THE SUPREME WORD, YOUR CREATOR, THE OWNER OF THE WORLD is pointing out to you that all the people that you killed and plan to kill have the **WORD** in them. As soon as you kill somebody that **WORD** would not exist again. That means you have driven **ME THE FATHER GOD** away from

MY HOME. Do you know that **I** live in every Living Organism and Living Creature? And if you fight against them you fight against **ME THE FATHER GOD.** Do you know that? Do you know that if you hate any living thing you hate **ME THE FATHER GOD,** especially human beings? All human beings are the Homes of **THE FATHER GOD** so, if you hate anybody you hate life. You hate your life in hating another life and you will answer for it. **I** want you to know that you will pay for the evil you commit. You will pay now and then and forever. People think **I** do not act. The reason it seems so is that there has not been enough information for you to use in addressing your life. Nonetheless, **I HAVE NOW BROUGHT THE UNIVERSAL UPDATE** through HRM King

Solomon David Jesse ETE, **King Solomon Spiritual Library FATHER'S TALK (GOD PRESENT) LECTURE REVELATIONS.** The reason that **I call THE FATHER'S TALK (GOD PRESENT) Lecture Revelations** is that the information is complete and clear and does not need interpretation and explanation except you use another language.

You must read at least Seven Lecture Revelations of **THE FATHER'S TALK (GOD PRESENT)** before you make any comment about this INFORMATION. Make sure you have access to at least seven different **FATHER'S TALK (GOD PRESENT)** LECTURE REVELATIONS that represent THE SEVEN SPIRITS OF GOD from the first day of the week to the seventh day of the week. Within that period, you will have the connection to know whether this information came from a human being or from **THE SUPREME GOD, THE FATHER GOD ALMIGHTY.** When you have seven copies of different **FATHER'S TALK (GOD PRESENT)** Lecture Revelation information in your possession and go through them then you can decide to make comment(s). However, the **UNIVERSAL UPDATE** today is to tell you that whatever is going on in your mind **THE FATHER GOD** knows. And if you stand for negativism you will not survive the shaking that will come into the whole universe.

C: **EVERYBODY MUST UPDATE HIS OR HER MIND NOW**

This is an opportunity for all souls to use to **UPDATE** their minds. How do you **UPDATE YOUR MIND?** You should decide and firmly assert that 'I am not going to be a destroyed soul and it is true that **THE FATHER GOD** created me. As **THE FATHER GOD** created me, **HE** created me for a good purpose.'

Even if you do not believe **THE FATHER GOD THE CREATOR WHO** created everything including you and gave you life, believe life. And know that the life that you are living is not your property. The air you breathe is not your property. You only see yourself in this world but you do not know how you

managed to be here so give respect to the actual cause of your life.
What is LIFE?
LIFE is this **PHENOMENON** that is talking to you now! **HE IS THE WORD.**
Do not complain, 'oh the English they use in this **FATHER'S TALK (GOD PRESENT)** Lecture Revelation is not very good. The grammar is not correct. There is mistake here and there'. What has that got to do with the information that **I AM** providing. **I** can speak in your dialect. If you come across any word you do not understand, ask **ME THE FATHER GOD** if you are positive and **I** will explain it to you in your dialect because **I AM THE UNIVERSAL GENERATING PHENOMENON.** I generate **UNDERSTANDING** and

WISDOM. **I** do not deal with language because **I AM THE SPIRIT. THE SPIRIT** formed all languages.
I do not deal with grammar because **I AM** THE GRAMMAR. Grammar means what you should not do and what you should do. That is the GRAMMAR **WE** are speaking now.

We are speaking the GRAMMAR of LOVE one another.
We are speaking the GRAMMAR of JOY, PEACE, HARMONY, KINDNESS, MERCY, ONENESS and EQUALITY OF LIFE and LIVE AND LET LIVE. That is THE OFFICIAL GRAMMAR WE ARE SPEAKING NOW. **I AM UPDATING THE GRAMMAR FOR THE WHOLE WORLD.**
I AM bringing this to your attention because some of you are

I Love You, I Love You Too

likely to leave the actual information and look at trivialities. Do you think **I AM** an English man? **I AM ALL AND ALL.** There are even languages you have never heard and you cannot find translation anywhere if **I** speak it. Do you know the meaning of this WORD *asa aminkensen? Asa aminkensen,* do you know the meaning of that? So, if you do not know *asa aminkensen* what is the meaning of grammar that you think you know?

Nevertheless, you should be able to understand every word in **THE FATHER'S TALK (GOD PRESENT)** Lecture Revelations. When a child talks, you the parents understand because you are the senior of your child.

I can decide to speak in Ibibio language.

I can decide to speak in Efik.
I can decide to speak in any vernacular.
I can decide now to speak in any other language than this English language here.
The English Language **I, THE FATHER GOD** in HRM King Solomon David ETE decided to use now is because HRM King Solomon David Jesse ETE's last life transit on earth was in the European country as King James1. When **I** finished with this phase, in future some of **THE FATHER'S TALK (GOD PRESENT)** Lecture Revelations will be delivered in Ibibio Language or Biakpan Language, where the original Hebrew language is spoken. Ibibio Language is the original Hebrew.

I will be using Efik or Ibibio Language to give **THE**

FATHER'S TALK (GOD PRESENT) Lecture Revelations then it will be translated into English Language. For now however, **I AM** using the English Language in honour of HRM King Solomon David ETE's last transit on earth as King James1.

When you are in the primary stage of anything, you use simple terminology in WORD. This is simple WORD that **I AM** using so that everyone will understand because this is a commercial and reference language.

English language was formulated to unite the whole world. It was to unite LOVE in PRACTICAL CHRISTIANITY through Charity work in England. That is why **I AM** using English Language now. So, if you come across **THE UPDATE** Lecture Revelation

USE LOVE TO UPDATE YOUR MIND.

Everybody Must UPDATE His Or Her Mind now with, **LOVE ONE ANOTHER**. Don't forget that **I** have no other love than **MY BYLOVE OF WORD** which is the order of '**LOVE ONE ANOTHER**.' You should **LOVE ONE ANOTHER**.

And you should not take advantage of anyone.

If you are the head of your country, you should protect your country. As a family, you should protect your family and their property. Protect your children. Do not leave your place to go to war at another place. Do not go to suppress people, march on them and stamp your feet on them because you think you are big because if you do, **I** will reduce you to zero!

Now! When you build a house where there is water, do not disturb the water. Is it because you are a human being and you have instruments to use that you decide to block the natural course of the water and divert its flow? **THIS IS AN UPDATE!** If you block the water and there is no other way for the water to flow along its natural course, remember **I AM** the water, so the water will find its way to flow. This is the complaint that **I** receive from all creations. Human beings give too much headache! Because **I** created you in **MY** IMAGE and LIKENESS, you use that as an AUDACITY to disturb other creations. You go to the bush and kill the entire trees but some of the trees that you chop down, you do not use the wood for normal business and living. You cut down

the trees and bank the proceeds.
What do you do with the money?
Trees are complaining about human beings.
Fishes are complaining about human beings.
Air complains about human beings.
Lands complain about human beings.
Animals, fishes, birds, every creation complain! And it is all about human beings. What in the hell type of a human being are you? The lot of you! What in the hell of humankind you are!
You bully everything!
Other human beings complain about big human beings.
What in hell of a human being are you?
That is why **I** have come with this **UPDATE.**

DO NOT KILL ANIMALS!
Leave animals in their territory. Leave them in their domain to be in peace there. Animals do not hurt human beings again! All animals mind their business. Previously, animals used to kill people but now when animals see you they run away. Why can you not leave animals alone? That is the complaint of animals. Birds are complaining about human beings because human beings go about to order birds and use them for witchcraft. Human beings order animals and use them in witchcraft to harm their fellow human beings. Animals are fed up with all that! Human beings order snakes to do evil. All animals including snakes are fed up with all that!

Human beings! LEAVE ALL ANIMALS AND ALL

CREATURES ALONE! MIND YOUR OWN BUSINESS!

Don't kill any living creature for food. You are to feed with living organism NOT living creatures. The living creatures are four, namely; man, animal, bird and fish. Three of the four living creatures are to develop and serve man. The three living creatures to serve man are animals, birds and fishes. They are to develop and serve man as angels. Man is humankind, the senior of all of living creatures created in the image and likeness of **GOD**. Humankind serves **GOD, THE FATHER GOD** then, other three living creatures serve humankind. That is what **I** put in place.

Humankind has freewill to do positive work. The other living creatures and other things have their ways of doing something for **THE FATHER GOD.** Humankind should look after their fellow human beings with LOVE. When these animals develop to become human beings they are to serve humans, **I** mean, the real human beings. You have to make life equally comfortable for them. It is not for you to suppress them and rule over them.

As **I** said earlier all other creations are complaining against humankind. To add to that, aliens meaning, those that come from territories outside this physical world, create their own havoc. They are foreign spirits that take assumed human bodies. **I** sent them here on earth on errands to help humankind but they came and turned to look like the real human beings because they saw that humans are stupid. There are many angels that came from other territories like the moon, the sun and other spheres to help humankind and to make life easy for humankind but when they came and saw that humans do not know anything and they did not know their left from their right and are sinful, they decided to lord it over human beings! All aliens should know it today that you have been reported.

All the scientists, technologists and senior citizens as big and important people are mostly foreign people. They are angels **I** sent to come and help humanity but instead of them helping humankind they rather lord it over them and rule them and squeeze them, making them suffer. They hijack the whole world! It is likened to someone sending you as a friend to go and help his children and his wife but when you go, you and sleep with the person's wife and impregnate the children too. What do you mean with that kind of behaviour? YOU ARE THEREFORE CALLED TO ORDER THROUGH THIS **UNIVERSAL UPDATE.** If you do not stop your evil ways, you will see what is going to happen to you. This means that if you are in a senior position and you do not treat the people under you well, ***THE GREAT UNIVERSAL CHANGE*** will visit you! This **UNIVERSAL UPDATE** is the **WORD** from which **I** want every human being to **UPDATE** his or her mind. If you have access to this information or any other **FATHER'S TALK (GOD PRESENT)** Lectures Revelations, make sure that you help other people to have a copy.

D: DO NOT BE LIKE THE LITTLE RED ANTS WITH SUGAR

This is part of the **WARNING! Do NOT Be like The Little Red Ants with Sugar.**
Sugar and other sweet things like honey and sweets attract the little red ants. When a jar of sugar is left on the dining table or kitchen or anywhere in the house and a little red ant discovers it, the ant goes and returns with other ants. The little red ants will form a route from their anthill or wherever their base is to that jar of sugar. All the hundreds and thousands of them would be trooping in through the route line that they have formed to feasts on

that sugar. These ants would be so engrossed and immersed as deeply as glue eating the sugar that they will be oblivious of anything else. Even if they see or hear danger coming, they would not budge because they have agreed to die with the sugar. You would beat the table and do everything to shake them off from the table where the sugar is but they will refuse to go. You would do everything for the ants to go but they would not go, until you clear the ants and put them in the fire or you spray them with insecticide and they die. That is the action that the evil people are looking for.

The world is very sweet for you. To be the head is too euphoric for you and so it goes into your head. A bigger country imprisons the smaller ones and lords over the people. King James1 of England started this when **I** send him from Israel. King Solomon of Israel ruled the people with a heavy hand so **I** transferred him and sent him down here to establish the United Kingdom. He still behaved as previously. **I** sent him to spread the gospel of Christ with **LOVE** but he went about collecting people's wealth to put here in the United Kingdom.

Then **I, THE FATHER GOD** advised him that okay, let the United Kingdom be the place for the custodian of Wealth for all those people that cannot control their wealth. Thereafter they could take back their wealth at a suitable time. Then he established charity to use as the forum to send the wealth back to their destinations. That is that and that is why he had to send the wealth back from

I Love You, I Love You Too

where it originally came from but they refused to do that rather they formed a gang to keep the wealth here in the United Kingdom and made the rest of the world to suffer.

I AM GIVING YOU AN UPDATE TODAY. Throw back the wealth that belongs to the United Kingdom (not the United Kingdom of England), United People, United Oneness, United Charity, United World. You must throw them all back! If not you will see the worst poverty that can ever be envisaged in the world.
I AM using the same mouth of that King James1 to give this information. King James1 is now HRM King Solomon David Jesse ETE who for that reason is now crying for wealth. 'Oh, **FATHER GOD** can I not have something to

do **FATHER'S TALK (GOD PRESENT)** Lecture Revelations with? Can I not have a bit of money to even publish or print **FATHER'S TALK (GOD PRESENT)** Lecture Revelations and also for the basic of things?' Ehhh! He does not want to pay for what he did. He wants to become rich! **I AM** leaving Him in that condition that **I** kept Him until when He finishes paying His debt then He would receive the miracle wealth that **I** gave to Him before. Now **I** keep His wealth in spirit, which no man can see. You cannot even kill Him. What are you looking for in Him to kill him? You cannot even begin to look for Him because where he is living now is nothing to write home about. **I** disguise Him because of **MY Will.** When he has done this INFORMATION, **MY** WORK up to a point then, the wealth will come. Nevertheless, physical wealth does not matter. What matters the most is spiritual wealth. Now if He says to someone, "Go you are blessed!" and when the person goes, they become a billionaire. **I** give Him the Power of the Spoken Word. His wealth now lies in the Power of the Spoken Word and the Power of His soul that follows Him for eternity whenever He is here physically, in all generations. He does not belong to anybody! He belongs to **ME** for **THE FATHER GOD.** Never mind that. Nonetheless, take the lesson that you will reap what you sow.

Now! Everybody! Thou shall not suppress another person. America, Britain, France, Russia and the rest of the whole world should unite together to spread the WEALTH, KNOWLEDGE and everything **I** give in this world to reach every human being.

THE UNIVERSAL UPDATE stipulation is:
Everybody in the world should have where to live as a normal good life. If you gather too much, you will have a little. But if you give it away, you will have enough to live with. That is **MY UPDATE.** The type of disaster that will go into the purse of those that make people to suffer in order to get rich is something that cannot be told by any human being. Write this today and keep. **I** strongly advice you that you should not be like the little red ants with sugar, that go about eating the sugar on the table and forget about themselves. When **I** give an order for you to stop

something that it would not be good for you in future and you ignore **ME** and continue to go to war, to suppress people, and establish evil programs to control people, **I** ask you, who are the people you want to control? Let **ME** make this clear to you. No matter what you do, you cannot control another human being. Every human being is **GOD**. You cannot force someone to do something. Have you not heard that you can force a cow to the water but you cannot force it to drink the water? **I** know all the evil programs that the so called governments of this world have established. Who are these governments? Some of them are from the few families that came from evil that got established and want to control every human being. You will never have control of any human being! Rather your evil ways will boomerang on you in spirit, soul and in the physical reality.

THE FATHER, THE LIGHT, THE WORD, THE FATHER GOD THE CREATOR OF THE UNIVERSE, the **ONE** that created human beings is the only **ONE** that can control human beings.

Now, **I** have sent so many spirits into this world. Do you know whom that person is, sitting next to you in your secret society? **I** can make **MYSELF** pretend to join your secret society just to frustrate you. **I** make **MY SELVES** into every plane because **I AM LIFE**.
MY face is there in your secret society. You would see that the person that does not trust you is **I,**

THE FATHER GOD. He does not trust your evil plans. Don't you see that when you train people to do evil, eventually that person would start to fight that evil you trained him or her to do and becomes stubborn against you? **I AM** that person. You will never know **ME**. The more you look, the less you see. That is **I, THE FATHER GOD THE CREATOR OF THE UNIVERSE.**

Since you cannot read people's thoughts, you cannot control anybody. Even if you create a robot or any machine for evil **I** will enter that machine or robot and fight against you. So, you better *quat!* And sober for the Holy Spirit of Truth.
THE WHOLE WORLD: OBEY THE FATHER GOD AND LOVE ONE ANOTHER and take

life easy. Stop suppressing people in different positions.

I will make sure everybody runs away from evil posts.
You would beg people to be prime ministers but they will refuse and say 'No! You take it.' You would beg people to be presidents but they will refuse. You would beg people to take the key posts and positions in this world and they would refuse and say, "No! You go and take it." You will see! Wait and see! Even in the Hades it will be so. From Heaven down to here on earth, it will be so. That is **THE UPDATE.** Do not be like the little red ants that got stuck with eating the sugar on the table, giving deaf ears to danger, until they were swept away and put into the fire and died. Do not be like that.

E: EVERY SOUL MUST RECONCILE WITH ME OR ELSE

How do you reconcile with **THE FATHER GOD?**
Join *THE UNIVERSAL SUPREME WORD SEASON CELEBRATION.* Recognize the **WORD.**
First of all you MUST recognize and honour the **WORD.**
I know a lot of people will ask, what is the meaning of this? What is the meaning of that?
The meaning of *THE UNIVERSAL SUPREME WORD SEASON CELEBRATION* is that **THE WORD IS PARAMOUNT** and must be recognized, acknowledged, appreciated, honoured and celebrated.

I mean that it is a must to **HONOUR THE WORD**. To **HONOUR THE WORD** is the first thing as the first fruit that **I** want from humankind. That was the request that the higher self of Adam asked saying that let what is done in heaven be done here on earth. You know that the **WORD** is **THE FATHER GOD** and the **CONTROLLER OF EVERYTHING, THE CREATOR.** In Heaven **I** ordered all angels and all souls to bow down for the **WORD,** which **I** use as **MY** Higher Self, as **MY SUPREME SOUL** of Nature but Lucifer refused adhere to this order. That is the reason you see Lucifer in the worst situation today. She is being 'CAST AND BAN' everywhere, here and there.

Now, **I** have come with the same thing. As **I** have established **MYSELF** here on earth, **I AM** establishing the same test as **I** did in Heaven. You must test your blood through this program. As a matter of fact the program in this PROGRAM is TEST YOUR BLOOD!
Every human soul must use this PROGRAM of *THE UNIVERSAL SUPREME WORD SEASON CELEBRATION* TO TEST HIS OR HER BLOOD.
I have given the directives on that regard but this is another additional directive on how to reconcile with **ME.**

Join HRM King Solomon David Jesse ETE to celebrate the **SUPREME WORD** and you are reconciling with **ME THE FATHER GOD.**

I Love You, I Love You Too

From the First October to the **Tenth October Every Year For Eternity** is the period mandated for *THE UNIVERSAL SUPREME WORD SEASON CELEBRATION*.
IT IS A UNIVERSAL CELEBRATION.
Make sure you register with HRM King Solomon ETE to have a record and then you can celebrate!
Celebration does not mean drinking alcohol.
Celebration does not mean you should fornicate.
Celebration does not mean that you should smoke anything.
Celebration does not mean taking any substances.
Celebration does not mean you should do anything at all untoward.

What the celebration stands for is for you to be happy! Sing songs,

be jubilant and make merry!
Exchange gifts! Visit people!
Your entertainments must be positive.
Make sure your family is aware that from:
FIRST OCTOBER to TENTH OCTOBER of every year for eternity is the period we HONOUR **THE SUPREME WORD OF THE UNIVERSE.**
That is the period we HONOUR **THE FATHER GOD ALMIGHTY, THE CREATOR OF HEAVEN AND EARTH AND THE WHOLE UNIVERSE.**

This has nothing to do with religion.
It has nothing to do with church.
It has nothing to do with anything but the pure celebration of you.
YOU and your family are the celebrants! EVERY HUMAN

BEING IS THE CELEBRANT OF THE SUPREME WORD CELEBRATION! However, you MUST connect your celebration to **THE SUPREME NETWORK** of *THE UNIVERSAL SUPREME WORD SEASON CELEBRATION.* You will do this by registering your name and obtaining a record. This record has nothing to do with anything. It only means your family. A family can have a record that applies to everybody in the family, which includes all the children that have not reached eighteen years of age. A family means a husband and wife and children under the age of eighteen years or any group of people that are related through blood or otherwise. When a child is eighteen years, the child is no more under your authority and must have his or her own record and File of Celebration of **THE SUPREME WORD.** So, from conception to pregnancy and to seventeen years and eleven months, the child can still register under their parents and celebrate **THE SUPREME WORD.** You can make donations as part of the celebration.

I have given directives on how the donations, that is, proceeds from the celebration will be shared.
The Government of the Land has a share.
The Christian world has a share.
The Muslim world has a share.
The CITY OF THE WORD, which for **THE SUPREME WORD** has a share.
The KING of Kings and the LORD of Lords, the Universal Shrine, The Adam incarnate, the last Adam, HE is the Universal Last Adam and the KING of

Kings and the LORD of Lords has a share in the proceeds of THE **SUPREME WORD** celebration. Then the rest of the shares go to the general meetings for all human beings.

Eventually ALL HUMAN BEINGS would come to know themselves that they are from ONE FATHER and that they are BROTHERHOOD. For now that they do not know these things in that they are all brotherhood, of one family is the reason that **I** share the proceeds like that so that everybody would benefit. When you celebrate, it is not just for you. You are also doing it for **THE SUPREME WORD OF THE UNIVERSE** that lives in every soul. That is the only way to celebrate the **WORD,** for yourself and others. Nonetheless, before you claim that you are celebrating

THE SUPREME WORD, first of all you must accept **THE SUPREME PRINCIPLES. MY SUPREME PRINCIPLES** are:

- **I, THE FATHER GOD THE CREATOR OF THE UNIVERSE** wants every human being to be a peacemaker.
- **I** want every human being to be merciful to one another.
- **I** want every human being to be kind to one another.
- **I** wish that every human being give equal treatment to everyone and treat one another equally.
- **I** wish you to be a righteous person.

Being righteous means that:
- You should show kindness.

- You should love **THE FATHER GOD**.
- You should love **THE WORD**.
- You should love your **CREATOR** with all your heart and Love One Another.
- Then of utmost importance is faith. You need to have faith without believing in any other thing other than **THE SUPREME WORD** who is your **CREATOR** and is capable of protecting you if you do not have any wickedness in you as such you are not wicked to anyone.

That is **MY PRINCIPLE** and it is **LOVE YE ONE ANOTHER**. When you do this, you will think well, speak well, hear well, see well and do well. **I** emphasize that you should think good thoughts, speak good words all the time, listen to and hear good things, see good things and do good things. **THIS IS MY UNIVERSAL PRINCIPLE!** When you agree to this, announce it to your family, to your church, to your government and all groups of human beings. When you announce this, it means that you have signed up to celebrate **THE SUPREME WORD OF THE UNIVERSE** and you will have **MY** HAND OF APPROVAL. The same applies to the rest of everything.

After signing up to meet these requirements and adhering to them, then **I** will automatically activate **MYSELF** in you. This is indirect way to return to the Garden of Eden. This is also an indirect way to inherit the Tree of Life, which human beings would love to do.

Having given you this **UPDATE** today, **UPDATE** everything for good. With this, the whole world shall be in peace. With this there is no more war between Christians and Muslims who are descendants of Isaac and Ishmael respectively. With this there will be no division, no demarcation, no segregation and no tribalism in the whole universe.
With this, everybody will be feeling happy and nice.
With this there will be no sickness, no death, no problems and no war.
With this **I** can call off disasters and problems that humankind is facing.

If you decide that you would not do this, then the angels that are around will be annoyed! When they see you ignore this information they will be greatly angered and really vexed! They will cause a lot of problems for you and around you. When ***THE GREAT UNIVERSAL CHANGE*** comes to your domain and you have not signed up with this program to **HONOUR THE WORD** then you will face untold problems. This is the **UPDATE** that **I AM GIVING TO THE WHOLE WORLD TODAY!** This is a direct way and indirect way to reconcile with **THE FATHER GOD** or else you face the music!

F: **THE TIME TO MAKE YOUR DECISION**

This is the crucial time for all human beings to make a decision. And **I, THANK MYSELF, THE FATHER GOD** that Princess Mfon Etteh and HRM Queen

Disem Solomon ETE are assisting with this program. Any other person that hears about this should find one way or the other to help HRM King Solomon David ETE to make sure that this information is circulated to all and sundry in any form. Promote this program because those who promote it **I** will promote them very, very high.

However, those who think they know a lot and see themselves as know it all, thus ignore this call to Honour the WORD including those who use bad words to discourage people, **I** will reduce them very, very low, to zero and below zero. And you know when **I** reduce you to zero and below zero that is six feet under.

And when **I** promote you, **I** will promote you to *higheristy* to be with **THE FATHER GOD.** And your nature and you system and your life will improve for eternity. This is therefore, **The Time To Make Your Decision.** You must make your decision now to take your stand to support or else you take whatever you see.

It is not too late but the sign of the end time is around. Check it! All sorts of problems are befalling humankind. There are disasters after disasters happening everywhere. There are earthquakes, flooding, hurricane, cyclones, fires but to name a few. There is a general unrest everywhere and in all situations and with governments. There is disarray everywhere!

As **I** said earlier, all natures have reported humankind that, humankind is disturbing their lives too much. Since you have decided to fight life, Life is now responding likewise and comes as hurricane, cyclone, fire, rain and every other thing that you see, to disturb humankind as they humankind disturbs other lives. That is the message you are hearing today, in spirit, in soul and in the physical.

What is a human being? Human being is a mere thing. Human being is a block, a building. If **I THE WORD** is not in man, you what can you do? All the people that claim 'I can do this and I can do that' forgetting that as soon as you take assumed body of a human being **I AM** the **ONE** controlling you via the **SPOKEN WORD**.

Also in this world there are some spirits that turn themselves to be human beings and come to this world to pollute the world. **I AM NOW GIVING THE ORDER**

FOR THE SEVEN ANGELS TO ARREST ALL THE SPIRITS OR ANGELS AND ALL THE PEOPLE THAT DEVIATE FROM MY ORDINANCE. This includes those that turn themselves to be something else as those human beings who turn themselves to be animals. If you do this, you will not be able to turn yourself back to be a human being again. All animals that voluntarily turn themselves to be human beings to inflict wickedness to man, you will not be able to turn yourself back to animal. One day **I** will expose the true nature of all creations. Those who are animals will turn physically to be animals. Those who have animal minds will also turn to be animals. You will see confusion everywhere in this world. Actually that is what is going to happen now. So, **I AM GIVING THIS WARNING! YOU BETTER *QUAT* because the HANDS OF JEHOVAH GOD AND HIS CHRIST ARE ON EARTH! THE HOLY SPIRIT OF TRUTH IS IN ACTION ON EARTH!**

G: YOU MUST BLAME YOURSELF

When you do not change because you have ignored this information, you should blame your life by yourself because you used the freewill that **I** give to you to be stubborn therefore, take a personal evolution to suffer.

In the time past when people speak the truth they were killed. This world has always been fighting against Truth but has the Truth died?

Do you know that Satan regretted the death of Christ? He agitated and regretted that if he had known that by sending the Spirit of Christ to Hades, it would mean that Christ would release the prisoners there, he would not have asked for the Spirit of Christ to go to Hades. There is someone that when you imprison, he or she goes and changes all the prisoners for good. Do you know that when someone dies and becomes a spirit, all their plans die that day? Do you know that if you kill someone in order to take that person's position, it is the worst thing you can do to yourself because that person has become a spirit-soul and would haunt you in that position.
Show **ME** a president that assassinated another to rule that stayed long in the office. Show **ME** someone that has killed

another to be rich that is actually rich. You will not have anything that you use wickedness to achieve. This is **THE WORD.** As a result, you better promote this information than hate it because if you hate it that becomes war for you. Tell the whole world that they should leave **MY** servants alone. The world should promote all the true servants of **THE FATHER GOD** and help them to continue with **MY WORK**. If you hate any servant of **GOD**, you hate your life. And that is the worst thing you can do to yourself.

Do not bring disaster to your people. Pharaoh fought against **THE FATHER GOD** and brought disaster to Egypt. Nebuchadnezzar fought against **THE FATHER GOD** and brought disaster to Babylon. So

many people who are human-animals fought against **THE FATHER GOD** and brought disaster to their people.
Every human being has individual salvation to pursue. Do not support anything that you know that is not good. Do not support anybody to go to war with another person. You must know automatically that it is not good to fight but you can protect yourself should anyone bring war to you. Do not support what you think is not good. If you are a woman, do not support another woman to leave her husband to go and sleep with another man. If you do your husband will also sleep with another woman. You can do something and bring disaster to somebody you do not know. Do not support evil so that evil will

not befall you because you shall reap what you sow.

Any country that goes to war, like Great Britain, United States of America, Nigeria and all the other countries that go to war in the name of United Nations have invited trouble to themselves. Someone goes to fight another person just because they can and asks you to come and support them and you go along and support that person then you have indirectly invited trouble to your country. When a blind man leads you, all of you will fall into the pit. Anybody that comes to you for war, tell that person to go to his own war or her own war for that matter.

United Nation is for good. It is to UNITE with **LOVE** and **PEACE**. United Nation is to bring everybody together and cater for everyone and house everyone. United Nations is to build a house for the whole citizens of the world so that everyone from eighteen years of age would have where to live and have work to do. You must also train them. Everyone must have work to do and lead a good life. Every human being today is another human being tomorrow. Every child born today is the future. That is the reason governments are there to give support and render help for the future. Everyone is to work for **THE FATHER GOD** as Servants of **THE FATHER GOD** and not to instigate wars and any rubbish program.

You do not need to go and live in the moon. Live here peacefully. Do you see the stupidity of humankind? The money you spend to go to space could build another country. You could build bungalows for everyone to live in. Some of the programs you spend lots of money to carry out are very unnecessary and satanic. These people that spend millions and trillions on programs to go to the moon are from the moon. Indirectly they came to siphon things from here to the moon. Just as the people that go inside the water to build things inside the water are from the water and by so doing they are indirectly inflicting suffering on earthly people. They are living here on earth and people are suffering and yet they go to build mansions in the moon. Is that not stupidity?

People are suffering here on earth. So many people do not have where to live, yet people are wasting money at different places and doing all sorts of rubbish.

That is sheer stupidity. It shows that those who support projects like going to the moon and going to mars and other places to instigate such activities are aliens from that territory and they came to destroy the world!
Hurricane, cyclone, earthquake and many other natural disasters are sweeping all these things out. You will see the result.

If human beings are stubborn with **MY UPDATE** and are stubborn with **MY WORD**, you will give **ME** no alternative than to take the world back to zero. And **I** can do that in just one second. In one second, **I** can call back everything to **MYSELF** called the *WHOLE*! When **I** call everything back to The *WHOLE*, all the houses you built on earth will be damaged. All your constructions will be damaged. Roads will be damaged.

Aeroplanes will be damaged. There will be no electricity. Nothing will exist again. Everything will go back to zero. **I** can use fire, **I** can use flood! **I** can use anything to call everything back to the ***WHOLE!*** So, you better not annoy **ME** to that extent because **MY** patience is running and really running out! That is why **I AM UPDATING THE WHOLE WORLD.**

AS **I AM LOVE,** do not use the good self that **I AM** to tempt **ME** as the people of old tempted **ME**. And they saw damnation! Nonetheless, since **I THE HOLY SPIRIT OF TRUTH** loves humankind **I AM PLEADING WITH YOU TO CHANGE FOR GOOD**. If you hear this INFORMATION from **ME THE FATHER GOD** and change, then all will be well with you and the entire world. If you do not change for good then blame yourself for what will follow you. **MY** paramount judgement is that **EVERYBODY SHALL REAP WHAT HE OR SHE SOWS.**

CONCLUSION A:
IF YOU LOVE YOUR SOUL DO NOT REJECT THIS MESSAGE

You are a child, an adult, a man, a woman, senior, junior, young; a president, prime minister, head of state, chairperson, a king or queen or any high post that you occupy, no matter who you think you are, provided you are a human being, or angel and turned to be a human, or fish turned to be a human or bird turned to be a human or animal turned to be a human; even if you are the real human beings

who are Human-Gods or you are human-animal, human-bird, human-fish, negative or **POSITIVE** person, God or no God, whatever you like to believe, you can do so. What **I** want you to do is this:
IF YOU LOVE YOUR SOUL **DO NOT** REJECT THIS MESSAGE. THIS MESSAGE IS THE **LAST** MESSAGE therefore, this is the time to act!
What **I** mean is that THIS IS THE LAST REMEDY. What **I** just said is the last remedy for humanity.

The **Universal Test** is for you to recognize in total acknowledgement **THE FATHER GOD THE CREATOR OF THE UNIVERSE** and follow **MY** Principles. When you, from a little child to the government sober and follow **MY** Principles, then **MY** peace shall be on you and you will see that this world will be safe for you to live. Without which, blame yourself for whatever you shall see and you should not doubt.

LET ME INFORM THE WHOLE WORLD, (unless you are spirit created to live in celestial realm then you can live there) THAT NO HUMAN BEING WILL LEAVE THIS WORLD THAT **I** CREATED AND GO TO LIVE IN ANY OTHER PLANETS! YOU WILL **NEVER** SUCCEED! You can go for a visit and come back, just like some spirits come here and go back. But if you are planning to go to live anywhere by building space ship and other paraphernalia to take you anywhere, you will vanish on the way! That is **MY Test I** give to all earth dwellers.

Fishes live in the water and other territories are already occupied. This earth is the territory for human beings. What you do here is for you. You MUST stay here and make this place to be good for yourself as a human being! And anybody that comes here must pass through the womb of a woman **FULL STOP**! If you are a ghost that hangs around here, on earth, you must go back. **I** will build a certain unique thing on this earth one day and everybody would see what is going on. **I** will expose all the secrets and secret things people do. People use witchcraft; magic and all sorts of things to do many things but all that is the WORD! NOW! **I** WITHDRAW THE POTENCY FOR ALL THE NEGATIVE WORDS!
None of them will work again!

No witchcraft operates again!
No secret society works again!
No matter the amount of sacrifice you offer for evil and the shedding of blood, no evil will work again! **I** render all those negative energies useless!
I recall the energy back to **THE POSITIVE SUPREME WORD OF THE UNIVERSE** with this program now and forever more. Amen! And from now if you hide yourself anywhere so that you would not die, it will not work again. You will see what will happen from today after **I** finish giving this Lecture Revelation. **THE WORD** can never go out and fail to fulfil on what it goes out to do, now and forever, more!

CONCLUSION B:
THIS IS MY UPDATE TO ALL HUMAN KIND

What you are hearing now and all other **FATHER'S TALK (GOD PRESENT)** Lecture Revelations are all **UPDATES** for all humankind. As **I** said, **I** kept this **UPDATE** in King Solomon Spiritual Library and brought it out to all humans in the same manner **I** used to talk to Isaac, Jeremiah, Isaiah and all the prophets of **GOD**. Because some human beings think that there is no **GOD**, they have also concluded that there is nothing like the Voice of **GOD**. **I AM** telling you now that **I, THE FATHER GOD** always talks. Every human being speaks therefore that is **ME THE**

FATHER GOD speaking. **I** talk through them.

What **I AM** doing now is to differentiate **THE FATHER GOD'S TALK (GOD PRESENT)** from carnal talks as the voice of the flesh from the voice of THE SPIRIT. This is **THE VOICE OF THE FATHER GOD THE SUPREME WORD OF THE UNIVERSE.** It is not the voice of an ordinary human being. It is not the voice of man. What you hear and you are hearing today is coded. This **WORD** is accompanied with **A UNIVERSAL POTENCY OF THE SUPREME WORD** and if you give a deaf ear to it, then you will see what will happen.

CONCLUSION C:
THE ONLY REMEDY

The Only Remedy for the world is to **LOVE ONE ANOTHER** and practice peace. All citizens of the world should take note that when you join in the celebration of **THE SUPREME WORD** and register for the program, **I** will make you a peacemaker so that there would be world peace.

No single human being can make peace.

America tried to make peace in the world and so also did Europe. They spent a lot of money in trying to make peace in the world, yet there is no peace in the world. This is because no human being can make peace. **THE FATHER GOD** is the **ONLY ONE** that can make **PEACE. I AM** the **ONLY PHENOMENON** that can make

PERFECT PEACE in the world because it is only **LOVE** that can make peace. So, instead of spending money to go to war, spend money on this information and **CELEBRATE THE SUPREME WORD** because **THE CELEBRATION OF THE SUPREME WORD** IS THE GREATEST CELEBRATION ON EARTH.
There is a secret to it though and the secret is this:
Every human being breathes the air and every human being speaks the WORD, therefore every human being is the CELEBRANT. And since you are the celebrant, what are you celebrating? **YOU ARE CELEBRATING LIFE!** It is just as when you celebrate your birthday therefore, when you celebrate **THE SUPREME WORD** during that period of

celebration you are indirectly celebrating your birthday. For this reason you should not hate life again rather, you should **LOVE ONE ANOTHER.** The reason **I** said that **MY** commandment is to LOVE ONE AND ANOTHER is that **MY SUPREME POWER** is based on **LOVE.** The reason why you must love one another is because everyone is one spirit but with plural lives.

This LIFE is the WORD and everybody speaks the WORD. If you do not speak the WORD, you think with the WORD. In the light of this knowledge and understanding, everybody must register with *THE UNIVERSAL SUPREME WORD SEASON CELEBRATION* program. You have to show your acceptance of **THE SUPREME WORD** by becoming a member to officially celebrate **HIM** seasonally, which is every year for eternity. Your donation does not matter. What matters is the acceptance of this program and your support. When honest people hear about this program they will not deny it or ask irrelevant questions. They will instantly connect to HRM King Solomon David Jesse ETE and start the program with Him universally. HRM King Solomon ETE started this celebration with His family but now He has to start it with the whole universe. Everybody on this earth MUST do this.

When you celebrate **THE WORD** you must not hate another human being that speaks the WORD because if you do, you hate the WORD and that is yourself. If you celebrate The **WORD** you celebrate yourself because that is the meaning of **LOVE ONE ANOTHER**. This is what is done in Heaven and it must be done here on earth too. When this is established then THE PARADISE OF **GOD** has returned to earth in all earnest and that is when you will see joy, joy, joy, everywhere! This is for the simple reason that if you know that you are the House of the Spoken Word and another person sitting down there with you is another House of **GOD** then, you share what you have with that person so that they will be happy as you are happy.

You would not hate anybody that the WORD lives in. You would not be jealous of anyone that the WORD lives in because this is the Supreme understanding that gives long life. Therefore, after decoding this understanding, you will then become one of the peacemakers called Children of God in Brotherhood of **THE FATHER GOD ALMIGHTY** then the WHOLE WORLD will become PEACEFUL and there would be no death because death was established by the sin of hatred.

Imagine the situation where people are happy and always sleep peacefully then a bomb drops on their heads. What is the reason for that? It is because of greediness, the big people stamping down on small people to siphon their wealth. What are you fighting for? What are you struggling for when you can only sleep in one bed at a time?
How much food do you eat in a day?
Why do you accumulate so much?

Why can you not extend your good life to everyone if you are a human-God?
If you are really a reasonable person and not a STUPID one, why don't you share with others? If you are not an animal that came to destroy life, why don't you share with others? How many houses do you live in? How many beds do you lie on in a night? How many women do you sleep with in a night?

It goes that King Solomon married one thousand wives. How many women did Solomon sleep with in a day? How many children did he have?
It was a miracle! You cannot live that type of life anymore! You have to concentrate in LOVE and in PEACE and on how everybody should enjoy their life. It is like a man who impregnates many

women thus has many children but can not cater for all the children. Do you bring life to suffer life? You cannot be a president that uses the government money to go to war. You spend obscene amounts of money to fight without thinking of the wellbeing and comfort of others. All the minerals that **I** buried on earth are to finance every human being on earth to live comfortably on this earth.
That is what is called *THE SUPREME FUTURE.*
That is what is called **LOVE ONE ANOTHER**.
If you do this, then you have signed up with **THE FATHER GOD ALMIGHTY** for PEACE.
If you do not do this, know that you and **I** will share the same one leg of trouser. We will each insert one leg into the same leg of

trouser and wear it together for trouble. The **ONLY** remedy is what **I AM** revealing today which is **LOVE YE ONE AND ANOTHER** by **CELEBRATING THE UNIVERSAL CELEBRATION OF THE SUPREME WORD ON EARTH.** This is **MY** Supreme Principle for All Humankind.

I, THE FATHER GOD THE CREATOR OF THE UNIVERSE says that anyone as any living soul of human being, whether spirit or angel that promotes **THE FATHER GOD'S WORD** that is, **FATHER'S TALK (GOD PRESENT)** Lecture Revelations or promotes any positive idea of **THE FATHER GOD** including *THE UNIVERSAL SUPREME WORD SEASON CELEBRATION* and many others and supports HRM King Solomon David Jesse ETE on all the positive things He is doing, then **I** will promote that person very, very high to beyond the sky. You say that 'the sky is the limit' but **MINE** is beyond the sky. The promotion will be beyond the sky, far, far above the sky.

For the other side, if anybody for a second asks silly questions, in a bid to suppress this program and **THE FATHER'S TALK (GOD PRESENT)** Lecture Revelations, then **I** will demote that person very, very low to zero and minus zero.

From this basis everyone can choose from the above options, the capacity in which you want to operate, now and forever more. Amen.

I Love You, I Love You Too

THOSE WHO HAVE EARS LET THEM HEAR. MAY THE FATHER GOD BLESS HIS TALK FOR ALL HUMANKIND, NOW AND FOREVER MORE, *AMIEN*.

THANK YOU FATHER.

THANK YOU FATHER

Chapter Three

FATHER'S TALK
(GOD PRESENT)
In the Name of Our Lord Jesus Christ, In the Blood our Jesus Christ, Now and forever More Amien

HIDU-CUM

THE SUPREME LOVE STORY
============

MEANS EYE-OPENER, THE WAY TO HELP THE LOWER MIND

"Love Is The Sensible Spirit Of Everlasting Clear Way"

There was a very powerful Queen who had a garden and this garden was very beautiful. The Queen did not want anyone to plant or harvest in this garden except herself. She suffered a great deal to maintain the garden in a very grand way. She grew all types of fruits, vegetables, flowers and anything that one can think of was inside this garden. Her daily meals including breakfast, lunch and dinner, all came from inside this garden.

Being a powerful Queen, who had influence in the whole community, she made law so that her garden will be secure and only she would have access to the garden. She did not trust anybody even though she had many children and many people in the community, she did not allow anybody to enter the garden. The law she made was so powerful that if anybody went near the garden, they would be imprisoned for G (seven) years. This had been going on for

I Love You, I Love You Too

years and she was happy and everybody stayed away because they were afraid of her.

One day as she entered the garden to take something the key of the garden fell. She closed the gate thinking that the key was still in her bag. Usually, whatever she took from the garden lasted for a week. She did not check the bag and continued to enjoy what she took from the garden.

There was a poor family living near the garden whose children played football. One day during the football game, the ball fell into the garden. They could not ask for the ball because they were afraid of being imprisoned for G (seven) years because this was the law and there was no variation. They were so afraid that they did not play again and they became sad and did not eat and lived a miserable life, due to the fear that if discovered, they would be held responsible and could be imprisoned for G (seven) years. Finally, the Queen's food ran out and she had to go to the garden to get some more food, and that is when she discovered that the key was lost.

She sent people to look for the key everywhere and to search whether it had fallen on the road and to peep into the garden as well. They came and reported that they did not find the key but they found a football inside the garden. When they told her, she called an army to go and arrest the whole family and those boys were sent to prison. People started to lament, pray and cry and begged but she did not listen and left. She could not enter the garden and started to starve as she only ate food from the garden. And since nobody could enter the garden, she started looking for help.

Finally, she was told of a prophet who could see vision so she asked for him to come and see her but the prophet replied that she should come herself before he could tell her what had happened. The difficulty was that, she had a law that she could not leave her throne to visit another person. She begged the prophet and said that she will pay any amount, even give him A/C (a third) of her kingdom. The prophet refused and said that his law was that he also did not leave his temple.

The situation became very difficult and nobody could do anything and the poor family was still in the cell without food. Luckily for the situation, the prophet had a house girl who was the daughter of a community member.

The prophet had made that girl pregnant and this was reported to the Queen. There was a law that if you pregnant a young girl who is not married to you, you and the girl will be killed. The Queen knowing that it was the same prophet sent a message that if he did not want to die he should break his law and come and see her. By now the Queen was very sick; she had C (three) days left before she would die. She could not eat from anywhere, as it was her law. She was unable to speak well.

The prophet said before he comes, the Queen must write and sign that the law of death penalty for making a girl pregnant was no longer in effect. The Queen called all palace members and changed the law and signed, informing the prophet that he would not be killed. The prophet also called all spirits and asked whether he could break the law of not going out because if he did not go to the Queen, who will save the community as he will be killed. All spirits and congregation agreed that he could go anywhere and he would not die. The prophet now visited the Queen who was on her deathbed. She will have died in two days.

The prophet prayed with his group and saw a vision that the key of the garden was inside a small hole in the garden and the only person that could enter to get the key was the small boy that kicked the ball into the garden who was in prison with all his family.

It was then suggested that a new law should be written.
    A: People could go nearer to the garden.
    B: Release the child and all the family.

C: Anybody could enter into the garden with the permission of The Queen

D: Anybody can use the key to open the gate of the garden permitted by the Queen.

E: Anybody can take any food from the garden with the permission of the Queen.

F: Anybody can eat the food that the Queen will eat permitted by the Queen.

G: The Queen can visit another person if necessary.

When all this was written and read for the Queen she had no alternative but to approve that this was the new way of living in the community.

Immediately they sent for the release of the boy and his family. They were freed. The boy was forced into the small hole in the garden to get the key. He ate some fruit as he was very hungry and took some to his family.

The next thing that took place was that the gate was opened and some food was taken and cooked and the Queen ate. The Queen became well. Then she was taken to the prophet. She had previously not gone anywhere, not even to church. She now became a member of the temple. When she became well, she called all the members of the community to the town center and changed the name of the community from "Law community" to **"LOVE COMMUNITY".** She changed the name of the temple to **"LIFE CENTRE"** instead of "temple" because that was where she got her life back. She named the family of the boy that kicked the ball into the garden **"HUMILITY"** " to represent **"HUMILITY FAMILY** in the community. She called the pregnant girl **"MERCY"** to represent "**MERCY FAMILY"** in the community because the prophet showed mercy through her. She called the person who opened the gate "**PEACE**" to represent "**PEACE FAMILY**" in the community. She called the person who plugged the fruit from the garden, "**PATIENCE**" to represent "**PATIENT FAMILY**" in the community. She changed all the negative names to **JOY, HAPPINESS, FAITH and HOPE, POWER, WILL, UNDERSTANDING, WISDOM, ORDER, ZEAL, STRENGTH, IMAGINATION** which are all the components that make the pillar of the Kingdom of God. This became the life of the community.

From that day, the community changed from Satan's Kingdom to the **KINGDOM OF GOD.** They lived in **PEACE** and **LOVE** and there was no more law. As from today, know that **I**

THE FATHER GOD ALMIGHTY AM revealing **MYSELF** through this Supreme Love story. Any person, family, town, village, city, state, country, continent, or any group that changes from practicing law of wickedness and evil traditions to **LOVE ONE ANOTHER** and use the afore mentioned components of God, becomes the **KINGDOM OF GOD** and is saved **FOREVER AND EVER, AMEN.**

In the Name of Our Lord Jesus Christ, In the Blood our Jesus Christ, Now and forever More Amien

THANK YOU FATHER
Chapter Four

FATHER'S TALK
GOD PRESENT
Melchizedec, Twenty-four Bartholomew FATHER Two Thousand and Eight (BD.OI.BOOH)

I Love You, I Love You Too

Wednesday Twenty-fourth September year Two Thousand and Eight (24.09.2008)

In the Name of Our Lord Jesus Christ, In the Blood our Jesus Christ, Now and forever More Amien

LIVE AND LET LIVE
============

(LEAVE PEOPLE ALONE MIND YOUR OWN BUSINESS OR ELSE)

Now **I** have a small talk to give to insert into **THE UNIVERSAL UPDATE** Lecture Revelation that **I** delivered.
The title is: **LIVE AND LET LIVE (LEAVE PEOPLE ALONE MIND YOUR OWN BUSINESS OR ELSE FACE**

THE MUSIC FROM ME THE FATHER GOD)

I want to use this opportunity to ask all human beings, all angels, all spirits, and all souls:
Are you the creator of spirit?
Are you spirit?
Who created you, who made you if you are a spirit or soul? Who made you? Since **I AM THE SUPREME CREATOR, THE SUPREME ALL AND ALL** and you are only subordinates and object souls, you must subject yourself to **THE SUPREME LIFE** and respect life, starting from your own life to every other life, especially Living Creatures. The living creatures consist of the three living creatures including man, making a total of four living creatures. To put it succinctly, the four living creatures are; living creature man, living creature

animal, living creature bird and living creature fish and you must respect all lives. The worst thing that you can do to make **ME** your enemy is the worst sin that you can commit and that is to kill.
Thou shalt not kill.
Thou shalt not destroy life in spirit or in soul.
Do not even be wicked to life!
Do not torture life!

This is a strict warning to all humankind!
You must be helpful to a fellow human being like you. Do not tamper with his or her life.
If you are a woman and you realize that you are pregnant after seventy-two hours after meeting a man and miss your period then it means that a foetus has formed and that foetus has become a human being inside your womb, do not terminate it or you will

answer for it. This is MY instruction for unborn human beings how much more those are that have already been born. As a human being, if you commit sin including the one that leads to death, you should know that the law is that you shall reap whatever you sow. DO NOT TAMPER WITH LIVE! Every human being that has life is a lifesaver, a life preserver, and has life guidance and life protector. You- as a human being you must protect another life in any capacity that you can. If you live carelessly and wickedly with another life, you will answer for it seven times, one hundred million times. **I** have not permitted anybody to have blood in his or her hands. DO NOT HARM LIFE.

Let **ME** declare this openly as **I** said before that LIFE IS **THE**

FATHER GOD. Exception of **MYSELF THE FATHER GOD** that can do anything with life, no one else is allowed. If you tamper with life, you are toying with what you will not be able to handle. Even if you call yourself Satan, even if you call yourself demon or you call yourself wickedness itself, you do not have the right to even be wicked to yourself, talk less of others. Are you **THE CREATOR**?
Answer this query about the aforementioned living creatures. Are you the one that created any of them? Can you tell **ME** about the living creatures **I** mentioned if you created them?
Do you make life?
Do you make blood?
Do you make water?
Did you create yourself?

I Love You, I Love You Too

Can you make life for even one second?
This whole world as big as it, grown to this magnitude; do you know how it managed to be the world?
Who made this world?
Who made air?
Who made the time?
Who made trees?
Who made animals?
Who made birds?
Who made fishes?
I AM talking to you- human beings, how do you have the audacity to lay evil hands to hurt a fellow human being like you?
I know you are evil!
I know you are Satan!
I know you are the evil one that is why you do not fear life. You do not treasure life. However, since you have declared yourself a wanted soul or human being or

whatever you are, and tamper with life, plan evil against life then you should remember that you do all that to yourself and you have to repent now.

From today! Anything you think, you think for yourself. Let **ME** use this opportunity to inform the entire creations especially human beings that whatever you wish someone will reflect in you. Immediately you think anything it will reverse one million times back into your system. So, if you have a wish in you whether in your spirit or soul or physically for somebody to die or for somebody to be sick or for somebody to be poor or for any kind of wickedness or problems to befall someone then, immediately such thought cross your mind **I THE FATHER GOD, THE SUPREME WORD OF THE UNIVERSE, THE**

SUPREME THOUGHT that you mess about with in you, then **I THE FATHER GOD THE SUPREME THOUGHT** will give you seven minutes to have a second thought. **I** do this became of positive children of **GOD** that Satan will tempt. If after seven minutes, you do not rearrange thought, then **I** will return that energy to you and your body and you will immediately to start to be hot and to really heat up because of the evil that you are thinking. Whether you are an alien or whether you are any type of human pretending to be human, but you are not the positive human God, pretending to be human, but you are fish, pretending to be human, but you are bird, pretending to be human, but you are evil, demon, **I, THE SUPREME WORD OF THE**

UNIVERSE, THE FATHER GOD ALMIGHTY make this declaration today via this WORD that if you wish anybody anything evil, anything at all bad in this world, whether you use your spirit soul, or use yourself consciously or any form to think evil about someone, anybody at all within seconds after the grace of seven minutes, **I** will direct the whole thing back to your system, from spirit to soul and from soul to physical reality.

If on the other way you wish someone good, anybody at all, for instance, you wish someone to be rich, you wish someone to be fine, have long life and any good wish you put through for any person, that same second you do that, **I,** reverse it for you instantly.

What you sow **I** won't allow it to germinate before you reap it. **I** put

it back to you immediately. That is **THE ADVANCED UPDATE.**
This is part of **THE UPDATE.**
Therefore all the nonsense must stop! One person carry's a gun to shoot the other person!
Who are you to carry a gun and shoot another person, and destroy another's life? Who are you to sentence someone to death?
Who are you to tie someone down?
Who are you to plan wickedness against someone?

This **directive** that **I AM** going to give is the only thing that **I AM** allowing Governments of individual nations to carry out.
If somebody kills another person that person should not be killed.
You are not the one to kill the person.
This is what **I THE FATHER GOD** wants any government of

this world that represents **ME** to do.

If anybody kills and destroys another person's life consciously, he or she is already a dead person therefore he or she must be killed, but no one should be responsible of his or her death; if you do, you too must be killed. If you find someone guilty of any fault, the punishment for such offence should not overwhelm the person's sin, because evil and wicked human beings hide under those situations to punish and kill many innocent people. That is why you are not **GOD** to judge and punish someone. Leave vengeance for **THE FATHER GOD.** If you would not agree to leave vengeance for **ME,** and you give someone a punishment that is not right or bigger than the offence committed, the remainder and double of the punishment will be for you too.

Governments represent GOD as a care taker in the world, to take care of everybody on earth. You have the right to only to do this under the Power of Government. You should build a city outside the positive area **and n**ame it **'THE NEGATIVE COUNTRY FOR WICKEDNESS' THE HELL ON EARTH'** for all Negative and wicked People to live until **I THE FATHER GOD** pay them, and they are dead by them selves. Make different sections for different kinds of wickedness and give them their passport to hell to live there. You must make sure that they do not have access to the perfect part of the world, which the Positive human beings are living there in LOVE, PEACE and

UNITY in the perfect **SUPREME NEW FUTURE**.

For those that kill someone; as **I** said you should not kill them because if you kill, you will also have blood in your hands. Build a place for murderers and killers and then send all the people that kill to that place. If they kill someone in the spiritual way, that others may not know but **I THE SUPREME WORD THE CREATOR OF THE UNIVERSE** knows all evil and wicked human beings on earth, so **I THE SUPREME LIFE, THE WORD** will make them to confess of their evils and wickedness by force. Do not allow them access back to where the normal people live. Make sure that you are truthful about convicting anyone of any crime. Do not allow any human being to tell lies against another person that will lead you to commit an innocent person to the NEGATIVE CITY. If you do so, such a person or that government that judges wrongly and mistakenly puts an innocent person there will pay the penalty and he or she would have to be sent to live there too. You must ensure that all your actions are correct and truthful.

MY ORDER IS THAT: WHAT YOU SOW IS WHAT YOU SHOULD REAP. Do not allow someone who should not suffer to suffer, because so many souls are crying today. The crying and wailing of the innocent ones is too much! People are not in peace. People stay in their homes and others would go to oppress them, to burgle them, bomb and kill them.

Nobody is bigger than another person in this world as long as you breathe the air. A child that is born today is equal to the person that is going to die today.

Therefore, since **I, THE FATHER GOD THE CREATOR OF THE UNIVERSE, THE SUPREME WORD** is your **CREATOR** and you breathe **ME** the **SUPREME AIR,** you are not more important than someone else for any reason. Not even because of money and its usage that you have established on earth. Not even because of anything else that you consider to be significant or outstanding that you have discovered and established that makes you any more important than another person that **I THE FATHER GOD** lives in. You must know that if others have the same opportunity that you have, they could be as prominent as you are.

The differences in human beings stem from opportunities. This could come direct from **THE FATHER GOD** or from what you do. Nature gives you that opportunity therefore you should not suppress those who do not have such a good opportunity as you do. You should not oppress them. You should not threaten their life. Do not kill them. Respect life! It is the same life that you have for yourself that others also have; therefore, respect that same life in someone else. Honour that life. That is the life every human being will live from now on till eternity as THE RESPECTFUL LIFE, THE LIFE OF LOVE, PEACE, UNITY, UNDERSTANDING, EQUALITY, ONENESS, MERCY AND KINDNESS as THE TOTAL LIFE OF WISDOM

with **ME THE FATHER GOD ALMIGHTY** ON EARTH!
If you are an honourable person as a respectful person in any level of life then the sign of you being such a big and honourable person that is a prominent and important personality, is that you should respect life and LOVE everybody. This means that you know what life is all about, but if you are opposite, then you are evil and wicked and you should be condemned.

I AM now giving this warning! It a SERIOUS warning to all living souls and human beings on earth that you must **RESPECT OTHER LIVES AND LIVING SOULS**! If you kill anybody today thinking that you would live after you have killed, then you are mistaken because you will also die instantly. You will not escape and your soul will suffer forever in the hell physically, spiritually and in the soul. The person you killed could be born before you. He or she could even be born before you died and also deal with you. So, what is the need and benefit to kill someone and fan yourself that you can kill?

This is the REMEDY and ORDER FOR THE NEW HUMAN BEINGS and THE NEW WORLD.

If someone offends you for any reason, whether in the capacity of the government or individuals of any kind, no matter who you be, approach the person, talk about it and then resolve that problem physically in peace, love and understanding. You do not need to fight with the person or to start war. You must avoid killing any soul in any form. If somebody says, 'I am sorry,' forgive the person. If there is any means you can be at peace or live in peace with anybody you must pursue that means. That is the order of the day NOW in the whole Universe! NO NATION SHOULD GO TO WAR WITH ANOTHER NATION. That stops NOW because all must operate with the principle of, **LIVE AND LET LIVE!**

A neighbour must not disturb another neighbour.
No human being should terminate another human's life, not even to commit abortion and kill an unborn baby in the womb. No human being should hate another human being. No human being should practice any wickedness of any kind. No human being should suppress another human being.

Everyone should be free and live happily on this earth. The cries of innocent people ring too much in **MY** ear and it will not be an easy ride for you if you do not listen to this **SUPREME UNIVERSAL UPDATE** and the **WARNING** therein.

That is what **I** came today to tell humankind.

LEAVE MY PEOPLE ALONE! LEAVE HUMANKIND ALONE! LEAVE ANY LIVING CREATURE ALONE! MIND YOUR OWN BUSINESS!

If you cannot help in any positive way mind your business. If you can render help positively, then help because that constitutes additional blessing for you.

From today! **I WARN YOU SERIOUSLY!** Do not use witchcraft, do not use talisman, do not use concoction, do not use any means including secret society practices, and do not invoke anything to harm life. Do not torture any life! Don't use anything on any life. **LEAVE PEOPLE ALONE!** Starting from yourself back to yourself, you have no power over life. That is SOLELY for **ME THE FATHER GOD, THE CREATOR OF ALL CREATION INCLUDING MANKIND.**

I WARN THE WHOLE WORLD! When **I** send someone to speak the truth, people hate that person, because they hate the truth. Any human person that hates the truth hates his or her soul of life right from today. You must help to tell human beings to continue telling the truth. If they threaten you that you would die because of telling the truth, and you stop being truthful because fear and stop telling the truth and being truthful, you will still die eventually so, their threats do not matter and should not matter to you. Therefore, you better stand with the truth and surrender yourself to the truth and **THE TRUTH SHALL SET YOU FREE**. **I** WANT EVERY HUMAN BEING TO DELIVER THIS TO ANOTHER HUMAN BEING. Pass this information to at least seven other human beings. Tell them that this is a STRICT WARNING FROM **THE FATHER GOD ALMIGHTY THEIR CREATOR.**

I WARN YOU MAN! WOMAN! **I** warn you that you MUST NOT have anything to do with blood again from today! If you get pregnant then give birth to that child! Let **I, THE FATHER**

GOD do everything in the natural way.
I created man! **I AM LIFE!** If **I** do not want somebody to live **I** will turn off **MYSELF** from that person. Anything that **I** wish it should happen to someone, **I** will make it to happen naturally. Make sure your hands, your mind and your heart do not associate with any wickedness in any form to in being wicked to any human being. If you do that you will put on the same trouser with **ME** and t**h**at spells GREAT trouble for you!
LET MY PEACE AND BLESSING ABIDE WITH THE ENTIRE WORLD, NOW AND FOREVER MORE AMEN!
**LEAVE MY PEOPLE ALONE! LEAVE EVERY HUMAN BEING ALONE!
LIVE AND LET LIVE!
PEACE! PEACE! PEACE!**

LOVE! LOVE! LOVE! ONENESS AND EQUALITY OF LIFE should reign in the entire world.
All those who wish **THE FATHER GOD HIS GLORY** and wish good for others will reap good things. Those who wish evil and any bad will reap bad things, according to **MY** instructions, NOW AND FOREVER MORE. *AMEIN*!

In the name of our Lord Jesus Christ In the blood of our Lord Jesus Christ Now and forever more, *Amein*
THANK YOU FATHER
Song

Leave people alone o!
Leave human being alone o!
Tell the whole world to leave people alone
You are not the creator of mankind

Thou shalt not kill one another
Thou shalt not disturb other people
Thou shalt not be a bother to anybody
Leave people alone o!
You are not the creator of man
Leave people alone o!

Leave someone alone o!
Leave people alone o!
You are not the creator of mankind

Thou shalt not destroy man
Thou shalt not wicked man
Leave mankind alone o!
You are not the creator of the man

I AM THE CREATOR OF MANKIND
I AM THE CREATOR OF MANKIND
Leave people alone o!
Evil, leave people alone o!

Leave someone alone o!
Love ye one another live in peace.
Leave people alone

I AM THE CREATOR OF MANKIND
Love ye one another o!
Leave people alone o!

Thou shalt not go to any war
Thou shalt not destroy man
Thou shalt not kill anyone
Leave people alone o!
You are not the creator of mankind

Leave people alone-o-oh-oh oh!
Leave mankind alone o!
Human leave fellow human alone
You must love one another
You must respect life

You must treasure life
Leave people alone o!
Leave everybody alone
If you can't help leave them alone o!

Leave people alone o!
Leave human alone o!
Leave creation alone o!
You are not the creator of mankind

Leave people alone o!
Leave mankind alone o!
Leave creations alone – o!

I AM THE CREATOR OF MANKIND

Leave mankind alone o!
Leave people alone o!
If you can't do anything to help man
Leave people alone o!

Leave people alone o!
Leave MY children alone o!
Leave mankind alone o!
Love ye one another
If you cannot love them you cannot help
Leave them alone o! oh!

Your duty my duty is to love life o!
To preserve life – o!
To treasure life o!
To be kind to all life and all human beings o!
Leave humans alone o!

I Love You, I Love You Too

In the Name of Our Lord Jesus Christ, In the Blood our Jesus Christ, Now and forever More Amien

THANK YOU FATHER

> **"THEUNISAL-SUREME SEACELION"**
> The Universal Supreme Season Celebration
> ========
> **"THEUNI-SUREME WORA THECRO-THEUNISE"**

I Love You, I Love You Too

The Universal Supreme Word
Almighty
The Creator Of The Universe
==================
WWW.COME4WORD.COM

THE OFFICIAL SITE FOR

EVERLASTING UNIVERSAL ALL WORD SEASON APPRECIATION

I Love You, I Love You Too

CEREMONIAL PROGRAM
=========

THE UNIVESAL SUPREME ALL WORD

I Love You, I Love You Too

SEASON
CELEBRATION
(GOD PRESENT)
SOMETHING MORE THAN
GOLD
IN THE HEART OF ALL MEN IS THE

I Love You, I Love You Too

WORD

THE WORD IS THE MAKER, THE SOLE ADMINISTRATOR AND THE CREATOR OF THE UNIVERSE. THEREFORE, ALL MANKIND ON EARTH MUST APPRECIATE THE WORD IN ALL CAPACITIES FOREVER

FROM EVERY
OA OF AO TO AO OF AO
(1st OCTOBER TO 10th OCTOBER.)
YEARLY IS

I Love You, I Love You Too

THE UNIVERSAL SUPREME ALL WORD SEASON CELEBRATION TO APPRECIATE THE FATHER GOD ALMIGHTY WORDWORDWWORDWORDWORDWORD

CELEBRATION!
CELEBRATION!!
CELEBRATION!!!
THE

I Love You, I Love You Too

I Love You, I Love You Too

ALMIGHTY FATHER GOD, THE CREATOR OF ALL THINGS BROTHERHOOD

IKOABASIKOABASIKOABAS
IKOABASIKOABA

**ORGANISED BY
KING SOLOMON
SPIRITUAL LIBRARY**

I Love You, I Love You Too

HRM KING SOLOMON DAVID JESSE ETE INSPIRATIONAL HEAD

IN THE HONOUR OF THE FATHER GOD THE CREATOR OF THE UNIVERSE THE HOLY SPIRIT OF TRUTH AND THE KING OF KINGS AND THE LORD OF LORDS

THANK YOU FATHER

KING SOLOMON SPIRITUAL LIBRARY

THE GOD

I Love You, I Love You Too

ENCYCLOPAEDIA WORD OF INFINITY

===========

King Solomon Spiritual Library, God Universal Information Centre Father's Talk (God Present)

WITH LOVE

Covered: **This BOOK,** e-book, software or software's, books, website, video, audio, idea or ideas, formula or formulas, manual or instruction manual.

... Hereby gives you a non-exclusive license to use the ... (THIS BOOK).

Some of the word here is coded with the (WORD OF SUPER HOLY AND INTELLIGENCE FATHER GOD ALMIGHTY)

Title, ownership rights, and intellectual property rights in and to the Website, Books, E-book, Audios and Videos, Shops and Store – e-Stores, Fundraisings, Celebrations and the supreme word seasons Celebration formulas and arrangement, Positive Inspiration, Holy (Fata), FATHER GOD ALMIGHTY POSSESSING SPIRIT in thought, in words and in did, thinking well, speaking well, hearing well and doing well shall remain in me and in ... The BOOK is protected by international copyright.

FATHER'S TALK (GOD PRESENT)

The message in The Father's Talk (GOD PRESENT) does not challenge any authority either individuals, groups or governments of any land or even any belief of any form. It is rather challenging the truth that is hidden from mankind. Therefore, any spirit, soul or physical human being who decides to challenge this truth shall have himself or herself to blame.

Key A
Any individual that reads any of The Father's Talk (GOD PRESENT) with faith; love and acceptance will experience immediate positive change in his or her life from spirit, soul to physical. If he or she accepts the message then he or she will be free from any evil.

Key B: PEACE AND LOVE

If you do not believe the contents of any of The Father's Talk (GOD PRESENT) it is possible through The Father's divine love and peace simply hands over your copy to a friend or somebody else that would like to keep a copy, or signing out from any of the website that connected to The Father's Talk (GOD PRESENT) KING SOLOMON SPIRITUAL e-LIBRARY without any evil and negative comments and you are blessed and free.

========

FROM THE DESK OF INSPIRATIONAL HEAD

Fees, Prices and Donations;
There is no refund on fees, price or donations since your fees price

or donations are using as a charity contribution to do administration work of THE SUPREME WORD, So please kindly read this first before you decide to involves yourself in any of the under mention of HRM King Solomon David Jesse ETE universal Inspirational Businesses of (GOD PRESENT) in cash, kinds and otherwise.

I CAME FROM THE FATHER GOD, WITH THE FATHER GOD, AND BY THE FATHER GOD TO ESTABLISH THE FOLLOWING:

Therefore, all distributors and contributors of The Father's Talk (GOD PRESENT), The Spiritual Advice, Healing and Counselling on General Live (The Universal Supreme Spiritual General Hospital), New Songs and Psalms of King David and Solomon, The

Word of **GOD** Processing City in Ikot Okwo or e-City online, The Trinity Celebration, **"OUC FUND"**, The Universal Bank Account For All Creations, **"ERUFA"** ETE Royal Universal Family, **"THEUNISAL-SUREME SEACELION"** The Universal Supreme Word Season Celebration To Appreciates THE FATHER GOD ALMIGHTY **"THEUNI-SUREME WORA THECRO-THEUNISE"** The Universal Supreme Word Almighty, THE CREATOR OF THE UNIVERSE should attach this information to all readers, website visitors, distributors, affiliates person/group, celebrant and celebrations centres, supporters and promoters, members, workers and voluntary workers, Ete royal universal palace committee, governments and many other centres as an agreement. Please kindly know that I am not answering to any physical human except **PEACE, UNITY AND LOVE.**

"THEUNISAL-SUREME WORA THECRO-THEUNISE".

I AM IN THE STAGE OF SUPER HOLY AND INTELLIGENCE FATHER GOD POSITIVE MADNESS OF THE HOLY SPIRIT OF TRUTH, ENYEN ODUDU ODUDU ODUDU ABASI MI OOO ZIM ZIM ZIM ASSASU, POSITIVE POSITIVE POSITIVE. UKEMEKE AKA IDIOK UNAM. Let the peace and blessing of the Holy Father abide with everybody who corporate with this divine Father's Talk (GOD PRESENT

I Love You, I Love You Too

**THANK YOU FATHER
BY
THE HOLY SPIRIT OF THE
FATHER GOD
THROUGH HIS SERVANT**
Senior Christ Servant
HRM King Solomon David Jesse ETE
Brotherhood of the
Cross and STAR
Eteroyal Universal family
Ikot Okwo The Great City of Refuge, Ete Community
Ikot Abasi LGA-543001
Akwa Ibom State Nigeria-W/A
Tel. 08036693841
Email: ksslibrary@eteroyalmail.com

**READ AT LEAST
SEVEN
LECTURE'S REVELATIONS
BEFORE YOU CAN MAKE
ANY COMMENTS**

I Love You, I Love You Too

In the Name of Our Lord Jesus Christ In the Blood of Our Lord Jesus Christ
Now and forever more
Everybody should have access and read at least seven **FATHER'S TALK (GOD PRESENT)** Lecture's Revelations before you can make any comments about it. If you do not go through at least seven **FATHER'S TALK** lectures and you comment you may make mistakes. When you make mistakes your blood will be upon you because you would have taken voluntary evolution to misquote **THE FATHER GOD THE CREATOR OF THE UNIVERSE.** If however, you go through any seven of **THE FATHER'S TALK (GOD PRESENT)** –

one of **THE FATHER'S TALK** stands for one Spirit of God, which means that **FATHER'S TALK GOD PRESENT** Lectures Revelation are witness by the Seven Spirits of God, which **I** use as the Seven Church of God and Seven days of the Week, Seven spirits of Creations in one Supreme energy of THE FATHER GOD, THE SPOKEN WORD. When you read seven **FATHER'S TALK** Lectures then, **I THE FATHER GOD** will reveal you as positive person. Then you will have a portion in **ME**. One of **THE FATHER'S TALK** will have a portion in you. Then you would know that this information came from **THE FATHER GOD.** The Father's Talk God Present is not a mere talk from a mere man!

I Love You, I Love You Too

**In the Name of Our Lord Jesus Christ In the Blood of Our Lord Jesus Christ
Now and forever more**

I Love You, I Love You Too

THE UNIVERSAL SUPREME ACKNOWLED GEMENT

'THE ONLY SOURCE AND REMEDY TO END ALL HUMANITIES PROBLEMS'

Join me to Celebrate; Acknowledge, Appreciates and give full RECOGNITION to

I Love You, I Love You Too

THE UNIVERSAL SUPREME WORD, YOUR LIFE FORCE, THE TOTALITY OF ALL TOTALITIES YOUR CREATOR, THE FATHER GOD ALMIGHTY, THE CREATOR OF THE UNIVERSE

WWW.COME4WORD.COM
Contact EMAIL:
hrmkingsolomon@eteroyalmail.com

THANK YOU FATHER

I Love You, I Love You Too

The title List of some the
Father's Talk
(GOD Present)

1: THE MANUAL OF THE SPOKEN WORD

2: THE MANUAL OF LIFE

3: INVESTMENT WITH GOD

4: ISO IBOT EDEM IBOT

5: THE CHARACTER OF THE NEW WORLD

6: HELPMANTRANS

7: UNDERSTANDING MY WORD

8: TRUTH, POSITION, POST AND NAME

9: NON STOP BLESSING

10: IMPRESSION

11: STAGES OF EDUCATIONS (SPE, SSE & SUE)

12: THE ENGINEERING OF LIFE

13: THE CONTENT PACKAGE

14: THE BUDGET OF THE NEW WORLD

15: DIVINE ATTENTION

16: THE BABY SPIRIT

17: PROMOTION

18: ADVANCE AND PROGRESSING MIND

19: THE TEMPLE OF THE LIVING GOD

20: I AM OK

21: THE SPIRIT OF TRUTH

22: THE PERFECT PERMANENCY

23: THE FATHER GOD, GOD, GOD THE FATHER

24: HUSBAND, WIFE AND CHILD

25: GOD AND HIS HARBINGER

26: LIFE EVERLASTING

27: POSSESS

28: MY MIND AND MY PLAN

29: AFTER HEART AND AFTER MIND

30: MY DECLARATION & STAND IN BCS

31: BEYOND THE HOPE OF FAITH

32: MENTAL STAIN

33: THE PRINCIPLE OF SELF HOLD

34: THE MASTERSHIP

35: HIDU-CUM

36: THE UNIVERSAL PARENT

37: ADVANCED YOU AND ME

38: THE GREAT UNIVERSAL CHANGE

39: THE PROJECTED MIND

40: INDESTRUCTIBLE BLESSED FIVE STARS

41: ASTROTS, GOD PRESENT I AND MY FATHER

42: SONGS THE COMPLETION

43: THE RIGHT BUTTON

44: <u>AKWA ABASI IBOM- ETE - DIRECTING NDITO AKWA IBOM</u>

45: THE DIGITAL AGE

46: <u>GOD IS OFFICIAL CHAMPION</u>

47: A TRUE WITNESS

48: MYSTERY OF PROCREATION AND BIRTH

49: <u>THE UNIVERSAL UMBRELLA</u>

50: THE FORERUNNER

51: A OF A TO Z (FIRST OF ALL)

52: MAN IN THREE CAPACITIES

53: <u>THE TRUE LIFE OF HOLY SPIRIT PERSONIFIED</u>

54: IN-BETWEEN THE FATHER & THE SON

55: DIVINE ARRANGEMENT & AUTHORITY

56: TWENTY FIRST CENTURY IS NOT FOR SATAN

57: THE SUPREME WORD SEASON CELEBRATION

58: THE MAXIMUM DEITY

59: TRANSFORMER TRANSMITTER AND WAVE

60: THE SUPREME FUTURE

61: THE BYLOVE OF WORD

62: THE SIGNATURE OF THE FATHER GOD

63: THE TWO WAYS

64: THE UNDERSTANDING OF LIFE

65: THE GREATER THAN SOLOMON IS HERE

66: THE CONQUEROR

67: THE SPIRITUAL GENERAL INSPECTOR OF LIFE

68: THE NIGERIA IN THE AFRICA
Part one

69: THE NIGERIA IN THE AFRICA
Part two

70: THE CREATOR AND CREATIONS PART ONE

71: THE CREATOR AND CREATIONS PART TWO

72: THE CREATOR AND CREATIONS PART THREE

73: THE SUPREME TEACHER

74: THE SPIRITUAL COVER

75: THE NIGERIA IN THE AFRICA PART THREE

76: THE SUPREME BELIEVE

77: CAST AND BAN (LECTURE IN LIVERPOOL)

78: LIFE EXTENSION MANUAL

79: THE SPIRITUAL TRAFFIC

80: THE VOICE OF THE CREATOR

81: MY OFFICE

82: LIFE SPIRITUAL FIRE EXTINGUISHER

83: INFORMATION

84: FATHER GOD FINAL ARRANGEMENT

85: THE LOVERS OF CHRIST

86: I LOVE YOU, I LOVE YOU TOO

87: THE UNIVERSAL SUPREME UPDATE

88: THE SUPREME ALTAR

THANK YOU FATHER

I LOVE YOU

Your name --------------------------------

I LOVE YOU TOO
FATHER GOD ALMIGHTY THE UNIVERSAL SUPREME WORD, THE CREATOR OF UNIVERSE

In respond to your LOVE LETTER I promise to love all human being including all your creations in spirit, soul and physical and from now upward all is well with me, in my spiritual life, soul life, this present life and life to come.

Email ---

Tel..

OPTIONAL

Address -------------------------------------

Postcode -----------------------------------

Country ------------------------------------

Signature--------------------**Date** -----/------/---
Respond Form/TUSWSCP/MS/

www.ingramcontent.com/pod-product-compliance
Lightning Source LLC
Chambersburg PA
CBHW032003220426
43664CB00005B/121